# EARLY SHIPS
# AND
# SEAFARING

# EARLY SHIPS
# AND
# SEAFARING

*Water Transport Beyond Europe*

Seán McGrail

First published in Great Britain in 2015 by
PEN AND SWORD ARCHAEOLOGY
*an imprint of*
Pen and Sword Books Ltd
47 Church Street
Barnsley
South Yorkshire S70 2AS

ISBN 978 1 47382 559 8

Printed and bound in England
by CPI Group (UK) Ltd, Croydon, CR0 4YY

Typeset in Times New Roman by
CHIC GRAPHICS

*Pen & Sword Books Ltd incorporates the imprints of*
Pen & Sword Archaeology, Atlas, Aviation, Battleground, Discovery,
Family History,  History, Maritime, Military, Naval, Politics, Railways,
Select, Social History, Transport, True Crime, Claymore Press, Frontline
Books, Leo Cooper, Praetorian Press, Remember When, Seaforth
Publishing and Wharncliffe..

*For a complete list of Pen and Sword titles please contact*
Pen and Sword Books Limited
47 Church Street, Barnsley, South Yorkshire, S70 2AS, England
E-mail: enquiries@pen-and-sword.co.uk
Website: www.pen-and-sword.co.uk

# Contents

# List of Figures and Tables

# Preface

Two-thirds of the world's surface is covered by sea; the other third has numerous lakes and rivers which, although sometimes acting as boundaries, were pre-eminently early Man's 'highways'. Since the Stone Age, water transport on lake, river and sea has been the prime means Man has devised to explore and exploit the world, link together its dispersed populations, and sustain trade and exchange. The raft and the boat (later the ship) remained supreme in that role until the advent of the aeroplane in the early twentieth century.

Boats are their own advertisement: there therefore has been a tendency for styles of boat building and methods of propulsion and steering to spread around centres of innovation, eventually to become regional styles. The author's intention is to describe what is now known about floats, rafts and boats of regions beyond Europe, from earliest days to the time that technical descriptions and illustrations of the world's water transport were compiled, and ships began to be designed formally. That change is not yet completed so that, in some part of every continent, floats, rafts and boats continue today to be built and used in traditional craft ways. Ethnographic accounts of such traditional water transport supplement the results of boat excavations and together they form the basis for this publication.

The book's title includes the word 'ships'. The 'invention' of the ship was important since there was a significant increase in vessel size, with all that implies for seagoing capabilities. The appearance around the world (but not everywhere) of vessels of sufficient size to be called 'ships' seems to have occurred as individual regions acquired the confidence inspired by Later Iron Age technology. Nevertheless, the term 'ship' in the title of this volume is misleading since the text demonstrates that Man has used the boat, a smaller and simpler form of water transport, for far longer than he has used ships. 'Ship' appears in the title: the reader will more frequently encounter rafts and boats.

Before the evolution of the ship, rafts and boats built of bark, reeds, logs, bundles and hides were not only relatively quick to build, but also matched the natural environments in which such craft were built and used, moreover, some of those craft could be used on seagoing passages when conditions were right. In tropical waters, for example, relatively lengthy sea passages were undertaken in large log rafts, especially after the introduction of sail. It was, however, only the planked boat (a relatively late invention) that could be increased to a size to become the ship that proved capable of traversing the oceans of the world.

The water transport of ancient Egypt is first discussed; we then progress eastwards around the globe to the Americas via Arabia, southern, south-eastern and eastern Asia, Australia and Oceania. The Americas extend over an enormous range of latitudes and climates, and have immensely long coastlines and numerous river systems but there are few published excavations of pre-Columbian rafts and boats. Nevertheless, much information about America's early water transport is available in descriptions and illustrations of indigenous craft encountered by fifteenth to eighteenth centuries AD European seamen. Subsequently, some of the water transport used by native Americans was further documented by ethnographers.

The continents of Africa (beyond Egypt) and Asia (east of the Urals, north of the Himalayas and west of the Gobi Desert) are two other landmasses that extend over a range of latitude and have correspondingly varying climatic zones. Rafts and boats were undoubtedly built and used in those regions from earliest times: indeed, recent aspects have been documented. Nevertheless, there are few published excavations of the boats of those part-continents and therefore there is insufficient data to compile an account of their early water transport.

Two of the regions included in this volume – Egypt and Oceania – were chosen not only because they are well-defined geographically, but also because each has had a distinctive boatbuilding history. Rising sea levels cut off Australia from the rest of the world at an early date so that the island-continent remained at an early level of technology which is best discussed in its own chapter. Other chapters deal with regions that have distinctive cultural – technological histories: Arabia, India, South-East Asia and China. Chapter 1 in *Early Ships and Seafaring: European Water Transport*, a companion volume to this one, deals with concepts and techniques that the reader may find useful when reading this text.

Each of the eight regional chapters, begins with a description of the maritime environment based, with permission, on a similar text published in Chapters 2, 3 and 5 to 11 of my *Boats of the World* (2001, Oxford University Press). This description is followed by an exposition of that region's main traditions of water transport. The third element in each chapter is a description of how such water transport was used: propulsion, steering, navigation and the like, including (where information is available) the identification of early landing places and harbours.

As the reader will find, there are great gaps in our knowledge, especially in those times and places before illustrative and documentary evidence becomes available, and reliance has to be placed solely on excavated evidence. The latter is not only rare, but also incomplete and it does not always present itself in an orderly and readily-understood manner. Nevertheless, as coherent an account as possible has been attempted for each region.

**Chilmark.**
**Easter Day 20.4.14**

# CHAPTER 1

# Egypt

The Greek historian Herodotus described Egypt as "the gift of the River Nile" since, without the fertility annually brought down this river and deposited as rich alluvium, Egyptian civilisation would not have existed. Moreover, the Nile may be said to have been responsible for Egypt's nautical development since it was the principle means of communication. In essence, Egypt was, and is, a narrow stretch of cultivable land on either side of the Nile stretching northwards from the first cataract, a natural barrier south of Aswan, to Cairo where the vast delta lands began (Fig.1.1).

This delta region formed the greater part of what was known as Lower Egypt where, in Pharaonic times, there were three principal Nile channels: Amun/Canopic to the west; Ptah/Sebennytic flowing north; and Pre/Pelusiac to the east. The river flow slowed within the delta and much of the silt it carried was deposited on the land, thereby increasing fertility. Nevertheless, the discharge into the Mediterranean could still be recognised out to a distance of 'a day's sail' (about seventy nautical miles) from the coast, where silt could be picked up on a sounding lead.

Within this exceptionally fertile valley, the technological achievements of Neolithic people led to a Bronze Age civilisation that rivalled that in Mesopotamia. The Nile was not only the ultimate source of Egypt's prosperity, but also became the principal 'highway' of the land. Mesopotamia was similarly dependant on rivers, but Egypt had the advantage that the Nile flowed northwards, against the generally predominant northerly wind: sail could be used to travel upstream, rather than towing as in Mesopotamia. In Egypt the phrase, 'to go north/downstream', was represented hieroglyphically by a boat

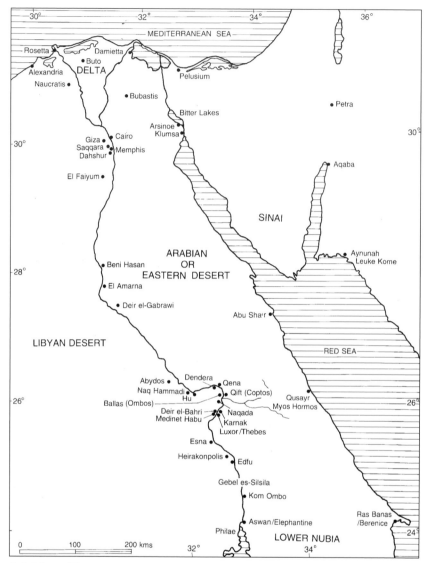

*1.1. Map of Egypt.*

without a sail; 'to go south/upstream', by a boat with a sail. Down the Nile, Egypt had direct access to the Mediterranean, especially to the Levant; up the Nile, then eastwards, through the eastern desert via the

2

Wadi Hammamat (a dry river bed), led to Myos Hormos/Qusayr on the Red Sea coast, thence to Arabia and eastern Africa (Fig.1.1).

In Neolithic times, papyrus reed was used in rope-making and to bind bundle rafts. Flint, also indigenous, was used to make tools. Subsequently, copper from the eastern desert (supplemented by supplies from Cyprus) and tin imported from Asia were used to make bronze tools. Egyptian trees, such as the Sycamore fig, the date palm and tamarisk, produced planks that were less than 6 m in length. This led to the import of Lebanese cedar which was available in lengths greater than 20 m and was easier to work.

**WATER TRANSPORT.**
The evidence for Egyptian water transport includes not only excavated boats but also representations and descriptions of boats ranging from the Neolithic (5000 BC), through the Dynastic periods (3100–332 BC), and on into Graeco-Roman times at the end of which, in 30 BC, Egypt became a Roman province.

Non-plank craft
Rafts with their buoyancy derived from ceramic pots, from gourds or from reed bundles were used on the Nile and in its wide-spreading delta channels in the seventeenth century AD and continued in use into recent times. This suggests strong roots, possibly as far back as the pre-Pharaonic times. Indeed, there are several depictions of what may well be reed bundle rafts propelled by paddles, from the later years of the Pre-Pharaonic period (before 3100 BC). A detailed, though fragmentary, depiction of what is probably a boat-shaped bundle raft is on a fourth Millennium BC linen cloth from a grave at El Gebelein in Upper Egypt (Fig.1.2): a helmsman and several forward-facing crew are shown plying paddles. Innumerable depictions of similar rafts, on pottery dated around 3200 BC, have also been excavated.

From *c.* 3100 BC, in the proto-Dynastic period, a distinctively shaped hull with high, near-vertical ends is depicted on an ivory knife handle from Gebel el Arak (Fig.1.3). On the same handle there are similar vessels but with curved hulls that probably represent bundle

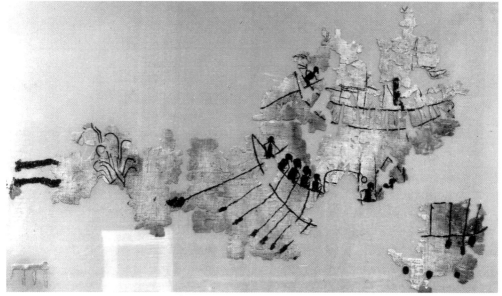

*1.2. Boats painted on a 4ᵗʰ millennium BC fragment of linen excavated from El Gebelein, Upper Egypt.*

rafts. Depictions of both types have been noted among petroglyphs on the Wadi Hammamat route through the eastern desert from Qusayr (Myos Hormos) on the Red Sea coast to Coptus on the Nile.

Although plank boats predominate in the iconographic and documentary evidence for water transport throughout Pharaonic times, rafts – especially those of papyrus bundles – continued to be noted. In Classical times, Strabo (17.1.4) mentioned individual large pots used as boats, and collections of smaller, sealed pots were linked together to give extra buoyancy to a light timber

*1.3. Two types of craft carved on the handle of an ivory knife from Gebel-el-Arak: in the lowest row and in the row one-third the way up the handle.*

framework. Bundle rafts were also extensively used in the Delta marshlands of ancient Egypt when hunting, fishing and fowling. In the eighth century BC, Isaiah (18.1.2) noted that Egyptian envoys travelled to the Levant in papyrus-bundle rafts, and Pliny (*NH* 13.22.71-3) reported their use in his day as Nile ferries.

Planked vessels 3100–343 BC

A feature of boats and ships excavated from Egyptian sites is the use of 'draw-tongue' or 'mortise and tenon' joints as plank fastenings. The tenons in those early Egyptian boats were unlocked and were held within their mortices by an interference fit. In the earliest-known, but of later date, eastern Mediterranean vessels, tenons were locked in position by a trans-piercing treenail thus producing a stronger hull. This method of locking tenons was also known to the Egyptians: indeed, some were used in the superstructure of the Cheops ship (see below), but not in the hull. Dr Cheryl Ward has argued that this practice of not locking tenons persisted in Egypt because vessels, built on the Nile, but destined for use in the Red Sea, had to be dismantled so that they could be transported overland along the Wadi Hammamat to the coast where they were re-assembled. Such dismantling would have been impracticable if tenons had been locked.

Illustrations and models from Egyptian tombs can readily be found depicting just about every conceivable building action, and every operational use of a boat or raft. For example, see Fig. 1.4 in which a man uses his foot to tighten the bindings of a reed bundle raft. Furthermore, boatbuilding scenes depicted in the Fourth Dynasty chamber of Rahotep at Medum, the Fifth Dynasty *mastaba* of Ti (Fig.1.5) and the rock tomb of Nefer (both the latter at Saqqara), and in the Sixth Dynasty tomb of Mereraka, include illustrations of the following techniques:

- logs sawn into planks
- planks trimmed with axes and finished with adzes.
- symmetry ensured by setting a line from end to end of the boat
- mortises fashioned with chisel and hammer

*1.4. Tightening hull bindings near one end of a bundle raft.*

*1.5. Boatbuilding scene from Ti's 5<sup>th</sup> dynasty tomb at Saqqara showing a strake being fashioned and fitted to the hull.*

- strakes pounded down onto tenons protruding from the strake below
- strakes fitted and aligned: the master shipwright checking the alignment with a ruler and plumb bob.

Other depictions in Nefer's tomb show a hogging hawser, led over vertical crutches along the centreline, from bow to stern, to pre-stress the planking against forces experienced when afloat, thus ensuring watertight integrity. Other early Egyptian seagoing ships (for example, those on a relief in Sahure's Fifth Dynasty burial temple at Abuir) are depicted with girdles at bow and stern, as well as a hogging hawser. By the reign of Ramesses III (1198–1166 BC) girdles and hawsers are no longer shown (for example, in depictions of Ramesses' third, and decisive, sea battle against the invading 'Sea People'). It seems likely that, by that time, Egyptian shipbuilders could dispense with such reinforcements because they now used locked mortise and tenon joints to fasten planking together.

Other innovations shown in these twelfth century BC depictions include: through crossbeams; a deck along the middle line of ships on which marines could stand in between the two files of oarsmen; oars plied through ports in the top strake; and a fighting top/lookout at the masthead. There was also a significant change in the rigging: the boom at the foot of the sail was replaced by brails. A loose-footed sail increased the master's ability to achieve optimum sail shape, and brails allowed him to match sail area to increasing wind strengths by hoisting the foot of the sail up towards the yard. Differential brailing, if it were undertaken, could have led to improved windward performance under sail.

### The Cheops ship

In 1954, the dismantled elements of a royal ship, dated to about 2650 BC, were recovered from an underground chamber at Giza, near the pyramid of Cheops (Khufu). This vessel is the oldest, near-complete, planked vessel in the world. After almost thirty years of research on, and re-assembly of, those remains Hag Ahmed Youssef Moustafa, of

*1.6. The Cheops ship of c. 2600 BC on display at Giza, near Cairo. The restorer,*
*Hag Ahmad Joussof stands on the right. (Paul Johnstone)*

the Egyptian Antiquities Service, produced an impressive vessel measuring 43.4 x 5.9 x 1.8 m, the bow rising to 6 m and the stern to 7.5 m: she is now displayed in a museum in the vicinity of the Cheops pyramid (Fig.1.6). The size and complexity of this venerable vessel indicate that, by then, Egyptians had probably been able to build seagoing planked vessels for some considerable time, possibly as early as 3000 BC when a range of woodworking tools were used by them in other trades: axes, adzes, chisels, pulling saws, mallets, wedges, bradawls, sandstone rubbers, squares, levels and rulers.

The Cheops ship was built plank-first, with the cedar planking being positioned and fastened together in five different ways:

- Projections from plank edges enmeshed with indentations on adjoining planks.
- Wooden treenails across plank seams
- Unlocked mortise and tenon joints across seams.
- Widely-spaced, individual lashings of halfa grass across seams

*1.7. The interior of the Cheops ship with temporary fastenings.*

- Transverse sewing from sheer to sheer: sewing holes within the plank thickness ensured that stitches were not exposed outboard and therefore would not be damaged when the ship was berthed (Fig.1.7).

During this vessel's working life, these features and fastenings would not only have resisted the tendency of adjacent planks to slide relative to one another (a movement induced by sheering stresses created when afloat) but also would have facilitated re-locating planking when fastenings were renewed, probably annually.

After the Egyptian shipwrights had fastened the planking together, the shell of the hull was stabilised by sixteen huge floor timbers lashed to the planking and by crossbeams let into the top strake. A massive, carling timber, supported by stanchions, was then positioned centrally on the crossbeams and lashed to them, thereby reinforcing the whole structure longitudinally.

Other buried vessels

Other Egyptian planked vessels, older than the Cheops ship, have been found, but appear not to have survived in such good order. The ritual of burying boats in association with the funeral of a pharaoh seems to have begun during the First Dynasty (3100–2890 BC) and continued sporadically until the Fifth Dynasty (c. 2345 BC), with an 'outrider' of five boats buried in Senusret (Sesostris) III's burial enclosure in c. 1850 BC, some 500 years after the Old Kingdom use of such ritual burials.

In 1947, nineteen boat pits, thought to be of first dynasty date, were excavated at Helwan, and, in 1954, six were encountered at Saqqara. Although boat remains were noted, nothing seems to have survived from either excavation, and the subsequent publications tell us almost nothing about the boats. In 1991, a group of fourteen planked boats were exposed at Abydos, to the west of the Nile, some 250 miles upstream from Cairo. These boats had been buried within brick 'coffins' in a second-dynasty (2890–2686 BC) funerary enclosure. The planking of these flat-bottomed boats had been fastened together by transverse sewing across the bottom and sides of each boat, as in the Cheops ship.

*The Dahshur boats* (Fig 1.8)
Five boats, dated to around 1850 BC, were excavated in 1893–1895 from pits near the pyramid of Sesostris (Senusret III) at Dahshur, to the west of the Nile, some 250 miles upstream from Cairo. Two of these are now on display in the Egyptian Museum in Cairo, and there is one each in Chicago and in Pittsburgh museums. The fifth boat can no longer be traced.

*1.8. One of the early-second millennium BC Dahshur boats. (Courtesy, Field Museum of Natural History, Chicago)*

As now seen on display, these boats are all of a similar size (approx. 9.5 x 2.25 x 0.75 m) and have a slightly-protruding plank-keel and a rounded transverse section; with a gently-curving sheerline with the stern higher than the bows. The short lengths of cedar planking had been hewn to shape, rather than bent. The three, longitudinally-laid planks forming the plank-keel of each boat are butted, end-to-end, and fastened together by wooden, dovetail-shaped cramps set into the planks' inboard faces.

Recent re-examination of these boats suggests that, after the boats had been recovered, the excavators fitted these cramps to replace the original, lashed fastenings. The three strakes each side are fastened together, edge-to-edge, by unlocked mortise and tenon joints and by widely-spaced dovetail cramps (formerly lashings). The ends of the top strakes, which do not run the full length of the hull, are lashed in position. These boats had no frames but each hull was reinforced by thirteen protruding, crossbeams, lashed in position and then tree-nailed to the third strake. Decking was fitted into rabbets cut into the upper faces of the beams. Each boat was steered by two quarter rudders with lengthy shafts, pivoted on the hull and on stanchions. Poles and paddles were probably used for propulsion since there is no evidence for oar or sail.

Hatshepsut's Punt ships

On a relief in pharaoh Hatshepsut's mid-second Millennium BC temple at Deir-el-Bahari, five Egyptian galleys, under oars and sail, are depicted approaching the land of Punt; they are preceded by a small boat with goods on deck. In a second scene, three of these galleys, loaded with goods, are seen leaving the port, while the other two vessels are still alongside, being loaded (Fig.1.9). The goods destined for Egypt include gold, electron, ivory, ebony, leopard and panther skins, monkeys, dogs and cattle, sandalwood, gums and incense, myrrh and myrrh trees – there were also several Punt people.

*1.9. A sculpture in Hatshepsut's temple at Deir el-Bahri, Thebes: two of her ships embarking goods in Punt.*

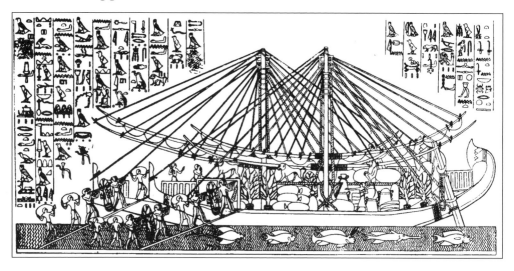

The longitudinal profile of the ships is similar to those on earlier depictions, but an unusual detail is that one has protruding cross beams. On another vessel, a hogging hawser (known in the Old Kingdom) can be seen, passed over three crutches, proud of the deck, and fastened to vertical girdles around both ends. There is no horizontal girdle such as appears to be on Sahura's mid-third Millennium BC seagoing ships. Like the Cheops ship, these Hatshepsut vessels have slightly-protruding plank-keels. The main structural feature that distinguishes them from earlier depictions is that, at both ends, there is a raised deck enclosed by 'guard rails'. The fore-deck is manned by lookouts; the ship's master and the helmsmen man the after deck.

Planked vessels after 650 BC
From the late second Millennium BC, when Phoenician shipbuilding techniques began to influence other eastern Mediterranean shipbuilders, it seems likely that Egyptian shipbuilders adopted the Phoenician use of locked mortise and tenon. In the early years of the 26th dynasty, from the mid seventh century BC, Greeks were encouraged to settle in Lower Egypt where they probably directly influenced Egyptian shipbuilding – for example, in the late seventh century, Pharaoh Necho II had triremes built for use in the Red Sea as well as in the Eastern Mediterranean. By that time, there was probably little distinctive about Egyptian ships: the Matariya boat (excavated from Heliopolis, north of Cairo) of the mid first Millennium BC not only has frames but also locked mortise and tenon plank fastenings. On the other hand, it seems likely that boats on the Nile continued to be built in the traditional manner since certain aspects of this style of building continued to be used into the twentieth century AD in the *nuggar* (gharab) planked boats of the Sudan, on the upper Nile.

## PROPULSION AND STEERING
Oars were excavated with the Cheops ship, and paddles are depicted being used in tomb paintings; the latter were also found with models from the Old Kingdom (*c.* 2600 BC) onwards. Oars, pivoted in

grommets made fast to a vessel's side, with oarsmen facing aft, were used in both the sit-pull mode and the stand-pull mode.

Fragments of early Egyptian sails (some with brail rings attached) have been excavated from Thebes and from Red Sea ports: these are dated from the first century BC to the third century AD. Those made from (S-spun) linen are thought to be Egyptian; others made from (Z-spun) cotton may well have been made in India – with them were deadeyes and parts of rigging blocks.

Until 2007, the earliest evidence for sail, worldwide, was believed to be an Egyptian depiction of a vessel with a single, square sail, set on a pole mast stepped towards the bow, painted on a Naqada pot dated *c.* 3100 BC: this pot is now considered to be a fake. Moreover, much earlier than any Egyptian evidence is the depiction of a vessel with a bipod mast on a sixth to fifth Millennium BC ceramic disc recently excavated from As-Sabiyah in Kuwait (see p.26). Later Egyptian depictions feature a square sail with a boom at its foot, on a bipod mast stepped about one-third the waterline length from the bow: this would, generally speaking, be compatible with sailing with the wind in the stern sector. On the Nile, with a predominant northerly wind, sailing southwards (upstream) with a following wind would have been the normal practice. By the mid second–Millennium BC, when a pole mast stepped nearer amidships is almost invariably depicted, it may have been possible to sail with the wind from nearer abeam.

Hatshepsut's Punt ships of the mid–second Millennium BC were galleys, that is, they were propelled by oars and by sail. Each oarsman, seated at a higher level than the protruding crossbeams, pulled his oar against what may have been a grommet at sheer level – except that oars are pulled (rather than pushed), the rowing action is not clear, but it may be that oarsmen began each stroke standing and ended sitting: if so, it is likely that their garment was reinforced by a leather patch on the seat, as seen on an Eighteenth Dynasty painting in Huy's tomb.

In those Hatshepsut ships, a low-aspect ratio rectangular sail has a boom as well as a yard, and is set on a pole mast stepped slightly aft of amidships. Each yard and boom is made from two spars fished together near the mast: both appear to be almost as long as the ship. The rigging is similar to that of earlier centuries: two forestays and a backstay; two halyard and lifts for both yard and boom. Braces and sheets are shown on only one of these ships. Unusually, the braces are made fast half-way along the yard and the sheets are even closer to the mast: possibly these are artist's mistakes. The boom, but not the yard, is shown lashed to the mast; with sail furled, yard and boom curl upwards towards their ends; with sail set, the yard becomes horizontal, whereas the boom remains curved.

In other depictions and models, the standing rigging consisted of a forestay (known from the Fifth Dynasty), and a backstay (known from Fourth Dynasty) with an auxiliary backstay that may also have been used as a halyard and/or a windward shroud. Sheets to the foot of the sail are sometimes depicted. In later illustrations, there is frequently a bowline from the sail's leading edge to the bow, with the helmsman controlling braces that run from each yardarm. Braces and bowline, and the use of a forked pole (tacking spar) to bear-out the sail's leading edge, make it certain that, by this time, Egyptian seamen were sailing with the wind on the beam or possibly from even further forward.

Pliny (*NH*. 7.56; 13.21) noted that the Egyptians wove the inner bark of papyrus stems into sail cloth; in later times sails were of linen. Sails were bent to a yard at the head and to a boom at the foot. In some depictions, this boom appears to rest on the sides of the vessel abaft the mast: constrained in this way, it would seem difficult to rotate the sail away from athwartships. There seems to be no evidence for the use of a parrel to hold yard to mast, and block and tackle are not illustrated, but first century BC and later deadeyes and rigging blocks for running rigging have recently been excavated from Egyptian harbours. In the later second Millennium BC, lifts from mast to both yard arms were rigged to give yard and sail extra support.

In Fourth and Fifth Dynasty depictions, the sail is generally of high-aspect ratio (taller than broad) and made of horizontal sail cloths. Changes to this rig appear in the Sixth Dynasty: sails become broader than tall (low aspect ratio); masts are lashed to knees, rather than fastened by trusses; and the yard is suspended from the mast by lifts from a position on the mast just below the backstay. If, as seems likely, the boom was longer than the ship's beam, the sail could well have been difficult to handle.

Depictions from the Old Kingdom (2685–2160 BC) show steering by a variety of means: paddle, steering oar, side rudder and centreline rudder. During the later third Millennium BC, two side rudders were used, one on each quarter, pivoted against a vertical stanchion: they were thus true rudders that were rotated about their own vertical axis. Centreline rudders, pivoted on the stern and against a vertical stanchion, are first depicted in the Sixth Dynasty (2325–2155 BC) and they become increasingly common by the end of the third Millennium BC. A small tender depicted on the mid-second Millennium BC relief in Hatshepsut's temple was steered by a median rudder. Hatshepsut's ships, on the other hand, were steered by a side rudder on each quarter: the lower pivot for each long shaft was a grommet on the ship's side; the upper pivot, a crutch at the upper end of a vertical stanchion. The tiller to control each rudder hung downwards from the upper part of the shaft.

## SEAFARING

'Pilot' was one of seven Egyptian occupational classes. After acquiring the necessary skills within the Nile delta, these specialists are thought to have graduated to piloting ships in the eastern Mediterranean and the Red Sea. Egyptian ships are known to have sailed the Red Sea from the mid fourth millennium BC onwards, and from the early Dynasties (3100 BC) they traded with east African ports for such exotic goods as incense, sandalwood and ebony. In the Mediterranean, Egyptian need of copper led to overseas trade with Cyprus; for tin, with Asia Minor; and with Lebanon, for cedar logs. Fourth Dynasty (c. 2600 BC) trade with Lebanon is mentioned on the Fifth Dynasty Palermo stone. By 1400 BC, Byblos, on the Levant coast where Lebanese timber for Egypt was embarked, was virtually an Egyptian port. During the Sixth Dynasty, an official of Pharaoh Pepi I was sent to the 'land of the Asians' to build a ship for a voyage to Punt. That ship-building site is thought to have been at the head of the Gulf of

Aqaba, east of the Sinai peninsula and the nearest Red Sea port to Lebanon and its cedars.

Egyptian inscriptions note that, between 2250 BC and 1450 BC, overseas military expeditions against Lebanon were also undertaken on at least three occasions. Moreover, in the Fifth Dynasty burial temple of Abusir there is a relief showing ships returning to Egypt with Asian prisoners, probably from the Levant. Herodotus recorded that, in the Twenty-Sixth Dynasty (sixth century BC), Egypt fought a naval battle against Tyre, and invaded and took Cyprus; subsequently, in 306 BC, Egyptian ships played a prominent part on the Persian side at the Battle of Salamis.

Voyages to 'Punt' (Fig.1.10)
From the mid third Millennium BC, voyages to 'Punt' feature in several texts, the earliest being in Fifth Dynasty Sahura's reign when Egyptian ships returned from Punt with myrrh, electrum and logs of (?) ebony. Later voyages are illustrated on a large-scale relief in Hatshepsut's temple at Deir-el-Bahari (Fig.1.9). Other Punt voyages were instigated by Hatshepsut's successors in the Eighteenth Dynasty (1503-1425 BC).

The location of 'Punt' has been the subject of discussion for over a century. In 1907, the renowned Egyptologist, Wallis Budge, suggested that it was on the west side of the Red Sea and also on the Somali coast west of Cape Guardafui. Later it was believed that Punt was on the east coast of Africa no further south than 10°N. In recent years, however, it has been argued that Punt was within the Red Sea region, in what is now Ethiopia; others have suggested the Gulf of Aden, on the north-facing coast of what is now Somaliland. The landscape, and the animals and trees that were said to come from 'Punt', seem to point towards it being on the southern and western coats of the Gulf of Aden, rather than in the Red Sea, nevertheless, opinion seems recently to have veered towards Punt being on the west coast of the Red Sea, possibly in the vicinity of the present-day harbour of Massawa which is thought to be the *Adulis* mentioned in the first century AD *Periplus of the Erythraean Sea.*

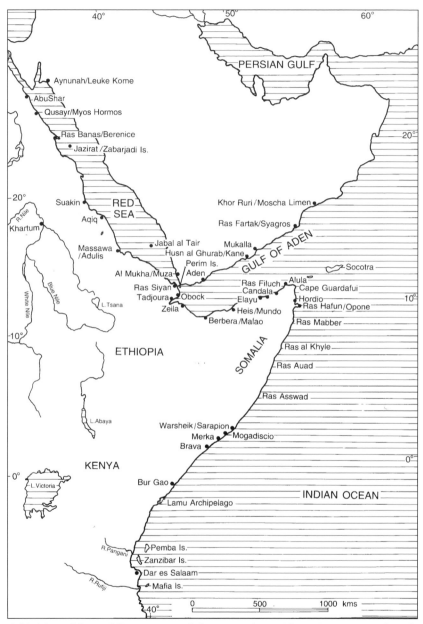

1.10. *Map of the Red Sea region and the coast of east Africa. Punt is now thought to have been on the south-west coast of the Red Sea, or on the south coast of the Gulf of Aden.*

18

Whether Punt was near the southern end of the Red Sea or on the Somali coast of the Gulf of Aden, it would have been possible for Egyptian ships of the Fifth Dynasty and later to sail to, and return from, Punt in one season. Leaving Egypt between July and September and delaying their return passage until March/April would have ensured a fair wind on both outbound and inbound passages. The final 500 nautical miles to *Myos Hormos (Khoseir/Qusayr)* of a return passage begun in, say, December, would have been against a head wind. In the early years of such voyages, galleys were used, so that difficult leg could have been under oars. Myos Hormos (a Roman harbour from the first century BC to the third century AD) had the advantage that it was relatively close to the Nile, thus overland travel was minimised.

Trade Routes (Figs.1.10 and 2.9)
The author of the first century AD *Periplus Maris Erythraei* was probably an Egyptian Greek experienced in sailing to, and trading with, east Africa, southern Arabia and the west coast of India. His handbook was primarily compiled for traders, but it also gives pilotage guidance to seamen on such matters as approaching and leaving harbours on the Egypt – India route, the set of currents and signs of approaching storms. There is also advice on hazards that might be encountered: for example, the *Periplus* warns that a passage along the Arabian coast of the Red Sea is "too risky" and "fearsome in every respect; since it is foul with rocky stretches". As the Egyptian coast is also hazardous, being strung with coral reefs, the *Periplus* recommended sailing in the middle of the Red Sea as far as *Katakekanmene* (the island of Jabal al Ta'ir), whence a coastal passage of some 200 nautical miles brings a vessel to the strait, Bab el Mandeb, at the southern end of the Red Sea.

The *Periplus* describes three main trade routes from Egypt departing from, and returning to, *Berenicê (Ras Banas)* or *Myos Homos (Khoseir or Qusayr)*.

*To the southern Red Sea*
For the Red Sea ports of *Adulis* (probably Massawa) and Hanachil Bay

19

(eighty nautical miles further on), the *Periplus* advises leaving Egypt in September, or earlier, when there would be a fair, northerly wind. From October to February, there would be a fair S or SE wind on the return passage, but only as far as 20° or 21° N. However, if the return were to be delayed until March/April, they would have had a fair wind as far north as 25° N, thus being able to reach *Berenicê* (Ras Banas), and occasionally *Myos Hormos* (Qusayr), under sail. Overall, this voyage would take about seven months.

*To the Somali coast*
The 'far side ports' were harbours on the north coast of Somali (the southern shore of the Gulf of Aden). These included 'Spice Port', probably near Cape Guardafui, at the tip of the Horn of Africa. The *Periplus* advises leaving Egypt in July when there would be fair N and NW winds. The Gulf of Aden would be reached during the SW monsoon when such winds would be fair for the passage along the Somali coast. The return passage, westward, was delayed until November when the change of monsoon would bring a fair E/ENE wind in the Gulf. The subsequent passage northwards, through the Red Sea, would have been as for the route described above. The overall time taken was about nine months.

*To the East African coast*
These ports were between 5° N and 7° S and included *Pyralaoi* (Lamu archipelago), *Menuthias* island (Pemba or Zanzibar, or even Mafia) and *Rhapta* (probably Dar es Salaam). No departure date is suggested for this route, but it seems likely that, as in the route above, they would have left Berenicê between July and September, so that they would be able to round Cape Guardafui with a fair N or NE wind, and sail along the coast of east Africa with a fair wind and current: they would have had until March to make Dar es Salaam. They may have chosen to remain there until September so that they could subsequently round Cape Guardafui after the autumnal change in monsoons in October. They would then have fair E and ENE monsoon winds in the Gulf of Aden, and fair S and SE winds in the Red Sea, reaching 17° to 20° N

in November or December. From this position they would have been faced with a lengthy, broken passage to Berenicê, against the predominant wind. An alternative would have been to delay this final leg until the fair winds of March/April.

The outbound passage to Rhapta would have taken up to six months, followed by some months in that port awaiting the change of monsoons. The return passage could have been begun in May, but this would have meant waiting for fair winds to make Guardafui. Alternatively, time at Rhapta may have been extended to September, thereby having fair winds to round Cape Guardafui in October. The final 500 nautical miles northwards in the Red Sea, to return to Berenicê or to Myos Hormos, would have been a lengthy and arduous, broken passage. Such a voyage – to Rhapta and return to Egypt – would have taken sixteen to eighteen months.

## PILOTAGE AND NAVIGATION

Passages in the eastern Mediterranean, the Red Sea and the Gulf of Aden, and along the Somali coast of Africa could all have been undertaken within sight of land using pilotage techniques to keep the reckoning of the ship's position. Indian and Arab seamen who, no doubt, had used coastal passages around the Arabian Sea (the north-west sector of the Indian Ocean) from 'time out of mind', probably also knew the direct route (Gulf of Aden to and from India) well before the Greek, Eudoxus, learned how to use the monsoon winds in the Indian Ocean. Strabo tells us that, in the reign of Ptolomy the second (145–117 BC), Eudoxus sailed to India guided by an Indian pilot who had been shipwrecked in the Gulf of Aden. Eudoxus was subsequently sent on a second voyage to India by Cleopatra III in 112 BC, but was shipwrecked on his return passage. From this time at least, techniques appropriate to navigation out-of-sight of land must have been used by Egyptian-based shipping on direct passages from ports in the Gulf of Aden to the west coast of India. The prominent headland Ras Fartak is likely to have been the point from which such ships 'took departure' for India (Fig.1.10).

The Egyptians early studied astronomy and mathematics, leading to the compilation of a calendar which enabled them to forecast the annual flooding of the Nile. In turn, this led to the use of stars as an aid to navigation on land and at sea: in the first century BC, Strabo noted that Egyptian merchants travelling through the desert at night navigated 'by the stars'. Such expertise was very likely to have also been used at sea to navigate out of sight of land. (see p.40–43)

## The Nile – Red Sea Canal

Having fleets on both of Egypt's coasts, and knowing that Egypt lay athwart the main trade route from the Mediterranean to East Africa and India, Necho 2 decided, in the early sixth century BC, to cut a canal between the Nile and the Red Sea (Fig.1.1). In the sixth/fifth century BC this was extended by Darius the Persian (522–486 BC). In Herodotus' day (mid fifth century BC) the canal was of a length equivalent to 'four day's journey by boat' and its breadth was sufficient for two triremes to be rowed abreast. Strabo (first century BC/AD) noted that the canal's breadth was 100 cubits (*c.* 50 m).and its depth was sufficient for 'very large merchant ships'. The canal left the Pelusias branch of the Nile slightly upstream of Bubastis, passed through the Bitter Lakes and entered the Red Sea near Arsinoe / *Cleopatris*. It seems to have been completed in the mid-third century BC during the reign of Ptolemy II Philadelphus (284–246 BC).

In *c.* AD 105 Trajan cut another canal from the Nile near Babylon (where Cairo now stands) to join the Necho canal near Thon, and extended Ptolemy's canal beyond Arsinoe to Klusna (near Suez). This canal was still working in the eighth century AD.

## Harbours

There were useful landing places (informal harbours) on Egypt's eastern coast in the Red Sea – for example, at *Myos Hormos* (Khoseir /Qusayr). In the Nile delta, at Naucratis and Alexandria, there were formal ports. One of Necho's successors, Amasis, granted the Greeks a site on the western (Canopic) branch of the Nile, which became Naucratis, the greatest of the sixth century Greek colonies. In time, this port became the only legal point of entry to the delta: if vessels by mischance entered another mouth, and winds kept them there, their cargo had to be transported by river and canal to Naucratis before it could be sold.

From 332 BC, Alexander the Great and his successors re-organised Egypt on Greek lines, paying special attention to commerce: they built new harbours and increased trade with Asia and with eastern Mediterranean lands. Alexander also had a new capital built clear of the delta, just to the west of the Canopic branch of the Nile, on a site that was protected from seaward by the island of Pharos. A causeway was built to link this island to the mainland, thereby forming two harbours, one open to the west, the other to the east. These harbours were protected to the north by Pharos Island and, to the south, by a third waterfront that bordered Lake Mareotis, a freshwater lake giving access to the Nile, thence the length of Egypt.

Since Egypt's Mediterranean coast was low-lying, in-bound vessels found it difficult to identify the primary entrances to the Nile delta. One of Alexander's successors, Ptolemy I Soter I (305–282 BC), therefore began to build a lighthouse on Pharos: it was completed by Ptolemy II Philadelphus (284–246 BC). This lighthouse had a distinctive, white marble tower – estimated to have been 455 ft (138.6 m) tall – which, by day, could be recognised from twenty nautical miles out to sea; at night, its beacon was visible out to thirty-five nautical miles. This Pharos light, the world's earliest, permanent lighthouse, was still working when the Arabs conquered Egypt in AD 642, but in *c.* AD 700 the lantern was destroyed, probably by an earthquake. Pharos proved so useful that, by the end of the Roman Empire in the west, there were thirty lighthouses in the Mediterranean and Black Sea, with others at Corunna in north-west Spain, Dover in south-east England and Boulogne in north-west France.

In addition to the Pharos lighthouse; Alexandria harbour had moles, warehouses, and ship-sheds. From the harbour, two canals led to the south: one to the waterfront at Lake Mareotis, thence to the Canopic branch of the Nile; and the second to the town of Schedia where import and export taxes were paid.

# CHAPTER 2

# Arabia

The 'Arabia' of this chapter is that part of Asia that lies east of the Red Sea, west of India and south of the Caspian Sea. In its earliest phases, the core of this region was Mesopotamia (today's Iraq) the land of the two rivers, Tigris and Euphrates (Fig.2.1). These rivers, flowing southwards from Assyria and the Anatolian highlands into the Persian Gulf, were not only the source of the fertility on which one of the world's earliest urban civilisations was built, but also gave access by sea to the Arabian peninsula coasts and onwards to north-east Africa, India and South-East Asia.

In southern Mesopotamia (*Sumer*), from the seventh millennium BC, crops were intensively grown and animals herded; further south, in the delta of those two rivers, fish were caught and fowl hunted. From the sixth millennium, irrigation of the land led to the establishment of permanent settlements; by the late fourth millennium, city states, such as Eridu, Nippur, Ur and Lagash, had emerged on one of the major rivers or were joined to one by a canal. Flooding risks were minimised and the fertility of the land was enhanced when the flow of these rivers was regulated by dykes and canals which also encouraged the use of water transport. The Nile was similarly regulated in Egypt at about the same time (3400 BC); subsequently, regulation of the River Indus was undertaken in northern India (*c.* 2500 BC), and of the Huang ho in northern China (*c.*1800 BC).

The co-operative work needed for those Mesopotamian enterprises led to the centralisation of administration and also to scientific advances: the measurement of time and the creation of a calendar; the invention of writing; and land measurement and mathematics. The need for resources such as metal ores, stone and timber by the city

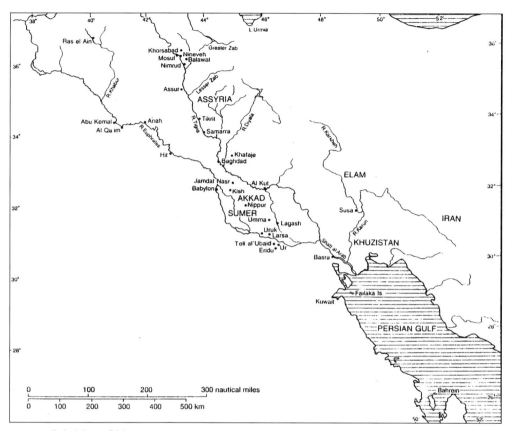

*2.1. Map of Mesopotamia.*

states led to external trade, not only with the highlands of Anatolia and Iran, around the headwaters of the two rivers, but also overseas via the Persian Gulf. The hierarchical nature of Sumerian society resulted in the import of luxury goods – overland from China, and overseas from the Persian Gulf, the Horn of Africa and the Red Sea coast. To balance these imports, the city states exported an agricultural surplus of wool, wheat and barley. Water transport was needed for both overland and overseas aspects of this trade: river craft to the north and seagoing craft to the south. States, such as Ur on the Euphrates and Lagash on the Tigris, became renowned for their international bazaars and markets.

**WATER TRANSPORT BEFORE THE 2ND MILLENNIUM BC**
In early times in Iraq, reed mats coated with bitumen were used as house walls. Furthermore, in ancient Ur, liquid mastic bitumen was poured into basketry moulds where it set into standard cakes which retained basket markings on their surfaces. Recent finds in this region of fragments of solidified bitumen with impressions of ropes, reeds and (occasionally) planks, have been interpreted, not as the remains of such reed mats or walls, but as the waterproofing, outer layers of bundle boats and sewn-plank boats. The oldest finds from the head of the Persian Gulf, at Subiya in Kuwait, include a ceramic disc displaying a vessel with a bipod mast, and are dated to the sixth millennium BC. Fragments from a Turkish site at Hacinebi in the upper Euphrates valley are dated 3800 BC. Finds from Ra's al-jinz, Oman, south of Ra's al Hadd, the easternmost point of Arabia, are dated 2500–2200 BC.

Some of the Oman and Kuwait fragments have barnacles on their smooth outer surfaces. Recent Arabian bundle boats had 10–30 mm thickness of bitumen, thus the Kuwait and Oman 10–40 mm thick, bitumen fragments, with impressions of bound reed bundles on their inner surfaces, are likely to be the remains of bundle boats, and those with barnacles must have been used at sea. The fragments from Oman with signs of sewn planking on their inner surfaces and barnacles on their outer surfaces are probably from seagoing plank boats.

These finds are, to date, the only direct evidence for early water transport in Arabia. The Kuwait bundle boat remains, of the sixth millennium BC, are much older than the world's oldest-known plank boats – those from Egypt dated to the early to mid third Millennium BC (see p.7, 10). The Oman remains of 2500–2200 BC, with sewn-plank impressions, are some centuries older than the Bronze Age sewn-plank boats of 1900–1800 BC from Ferriby on the north coast of the Humber Estuary in eastern England, but are not as old as the earliest Egyptian planked boats (see p.10).

Until those recent finds of bitumen fragments, the evidence for Arabian water transport, from the mid seventh to the early fourth Millennium BC, was entirely iconographic. Vertical lines across a craft's hull, on some of the models and drawings, most likely represent bindings around the reed bundles that form a bundle raft. Other representations have been interpreted, with less certainty, as elliptically-shaped, hide boats. Evidence for riverine and maritime activity increases from the mid third millennium BC: there are models, depictions and descriptions of water transport. In 2450 BC Ur-Nanshe of Lagash recorded on a stele that ships from Telmun/Dilmun brought timber from foreign lands. In 2350 BC Akkadians from north of Sumer overran the Sumeri, and Sargon, their ruler, proclaimed on stele and statue that ships destined for, or from, Meluhha, Makkan/Magan and Telmun/Dilmun were moored in the harbour near his capital. 'Meluhha' is thought to have been the Harappan lands of the Indus valley and the Gujarat coast. 'Makkan'/'Magan' was probably at the mouth of the Persia Gulf, on both sides of the Gulf of Oman. 'Telmun'/'Dilmun' is said, in the Flood myth, to be the place where the sun rises. In south Sumeria the river flows generally south-east towards the risen sun, the direction from which overseas goods would have come to Sumeria. Telmun/Dilmun may therefore have been the island of Bahrain and the adjacent coastal lands.

Information about Sumarian and Akkadian water transport has been found in numerous documents investigated by Salonen who deduced that, by the later third millennium BC, paddled, poled, rowed or towed wooden boats were used on the rivers and canals of Mesopotamia. The largest oared boat mentioned had a crew of eleven, while towing teams varied from two to eighteen men. Daily distances under tow ranged from six to twelve miles upstream, to eighteen to twenty-two miles downstream.

In 2300 BC, Sargon of Akkad proclaimed that he had been placed in a river as a baby in a rush basket made watertight with bitumen – such a basket would probably have been made of reed bundles linked by coiled basketry. Boats made watertight with bitumen are mentioned by later rulers and by Classical authors such as Herodotus, Strabo and Pliny. A number of early models and figures of boats, with flat bottoms and high rising ends, may also represent reed bundle boats.

Those recent finds of solidified bitumen with impressions of reed bundles on one side and barnacles on the other (see p.26)  show that bundle boats (not merely rafts) were being built in this region in the sixth millennium BC, and probably earlier.

Today, two distinct shapes of bundle boats are built: the boat-shaped *zaima* and *jillabie*; and the rounded *quffa*. Both types are built of reed bundles linked by coiled basketry, with light willows inserted to stiffen the structure. The linked-together bundles are then coated externally with bitumen to produce a watertight hull. It is not unreasonable to consider that similar boats may have been used 8,000 year ago in Mesopotamia.

In the light of the, admittedly intermittent, evidence it appears that, in the trade that developed in the Persian Gulf from the third millennium BC onwards, three types of water transport were used: on rivers and coastal passages – boat-shaped log rafts and bundle boats propelled by paddle and pole; seagoing – planked craft, possibly with a single square sail.

**WATER TRANSPORT IN THE 2ND & 1ST MILLENNIUM BC**
Thirty years ago, a useful catalogue of illustrations, dated between *c.* 2000 BC and the sixth century BC, of Mesopotamian floats, rafts, and boats was published by de Graeve.

Floats
Swimmers, using pot floats and hide floats to increase their natural buoyancy, are depicted on a ninth century BC illustration. In a seventh century depiction a large hide float is used by a man guiding a float-raft from astern (Fig.2.2). Other illustrations depict methods of making such floats: the goat, sheep or bullock skin is separated from the body; the hair or wool is scraped off, the hide dressed and all openings except one are sealed by tying. Small floats were then inflated through one of the forelegs, larger ones through the neck.

Buoyed rafts and Log rafts
Buoyed rafts (*kelek*), made of a number of hide floats linked by a framework of light poles, are used in Mesopotamia today (Fig.2.3.) They are depicted in de Graeve's catalogue on two reliefs from the

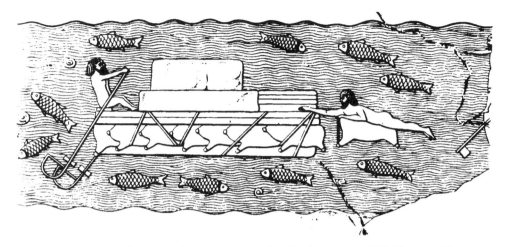

*2.2. A loaded, buoyed raft under oars, with a third man, on a hide float, guiding the raft from the stern. From the Palace of Sennacherib of c. 700 BC.*

reign of Sennacherib (705–681 BC): on one, carrying people; on the other, two large blocks of stone (Fig.2.2). Such rafts were propelled by two oarsmen sitting at the forward end of the raft each pulling an oar, with a third man on a float, swimming astern. The use of such float-rafts was noted from the fourth century BC and on through the Roman period. A raft depicted in another of de Graeve's illustrations consists of four logs bound together; onboard is a large, inflated hide float.

Bundle rafts and boats.
There are a number of illustrations of boat-shaped bundle rafts in de Graeve's catalogue in which bundle binding lines across the hull are clearly depicted: for example on an early seventh century illustration of an Assyrian attack on the marsh dwellers of southern Mesopotamia. Some of these rafts are simple flat ones (marsh dwellers?); others have strongly up-turned ends (Assyrians?). Some are poled from the bow, from the stern or from amidships; others are propelled by oars pulled from a sitting position near the bow; yet again, some are towed from the land.

Today there are two forms of Mesopotamian bundle boat: rounded ones – *quffa* (Fig.2.3); and boat-shaped ones – *zaima* or *jillabie* (Fig.2.4). Both types are built of reed bundles bound into shape by coiled basketry; they are then strengthened with a light wooden framing and made watertight by applying bitumen externally. These hulls therefore have a smooth outer finish and bundle bindings are not visible. Ancient illustrations of elongated bundle boats are thus difficult to distinguish from those of planked boats since there appears to be no Mesopotamian tradition of identifying planked boats by depicting planking runs as horizontal lines.

*2.3. A large, early-20th century, buoyed raft (kelek) and two round, bundle boats (quffa) at Baghdad.*

Round bundle boats (*quffa*) were described in the eighteenth century as: "baskets made of reeds, perfectly round – daubed on the outside and the bottom with bitumen". In the de Graeve corpus, round bundle boats are depicted in outline only.

*2.4. A 20th century, elongated, bundle boat (zaima) in the southern Iraq marshes.*

Hide boats

Hide boats are built and used in Mesopotamia today. A possible, early reference to them is in a *c.* 2000 BC inscription in Ure that includes hide and split willow in a list of boatbuilding materials. The round form of hide boat is depicted in the de Graeve corpus with 'patchwork' marks on its hull, as seen on the *c.* 700 BC bas reliefs of Sennacherib (Fig.2.5). Such boats were made from several hides and have a reinforced rim. They are generally propelled by men who stand, sit or kneel in one part of the boat, and, because round boats do not have a fixed bow or stern, that end temporarily becomes the bow (if pulling oars or paddling), or the stern (if oars are pushed). In the Sennacherib depictions, however, there are two oarsmen at both 'ends' of the boat, each pair being at the beginning of a stroke pulling an oar against a pivot: each pair is thus depicted pulling against the other – an 'artist's mistake'? A solution may be that one pair should be pushing oars on the power stroke, rather than pulling, and they should have been depicted at the beginning of that stroke – the two pairs would then be synchronised; furthermore, the end at which oarsmen were pulling would become the bow. In a round boat propelled by oars rather than paddles, it would seem likely that the necessity for pivots and oarsmen's seats (Fig.2.5) to be fastened to the hull would effectively define the bow and stern of the boat, although those ends would not, by themselves, be recognisable.

*2.5. A hide boat depicted in Sennacherib's palace of c. 700 BC. (The British Museum)*

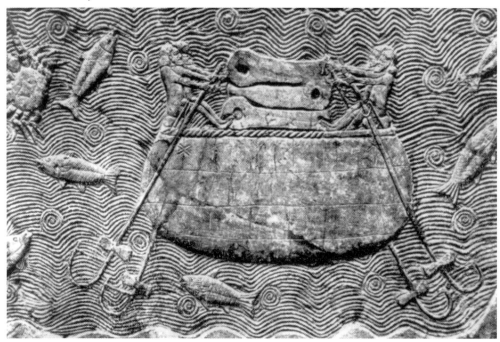

When Herodotus (1:194) visited Babylon in the fifth century BC, he noted round boats of hide stretched over a framework of withies. These had been built in Armenia, he was told, and brought down the Euphrates carrying casks of wine and a donkey on straw dunnage, propelled by two standing paddlers, one at each end. After unloading their cargo in Babylon, the boats were dismantled (because the strong current made it impossible to paddle upstream), the framing and the straw dunnage sold, and the hides loaded on to the donkey for carriage back to Armenia. In early twentieth century Baghdad, float rafts were similarly dismantled (a practice also known in China – see p.109): this has led some scholars to argue that Herodotus confused the hide boat with the float raft. There is no reason to think that hide boats could not be used as Herodotus described: indeed, in the nineteenth century, they were so used in southern India.

Logboats
Because there were few suitable trees in Arabia, logboats are scarcely known. There is one recorded observation from antiquity: in the fourth century AD, Amorianus (24.4.8) noted *monoxylon* on the Euphrates. These may have been imported as they have been in recent times when teak logboats were exported to Arabia from the Malabar coast of India.

Planked Boats
In the first century BC/AD, Strabo (16.1.11) stressed that Mesopotamia had little timber for boatbuilding. Nevertheless, Alexander had built boats in Babylonia from Cypress trees. Moreover mulberry trees grew in northern Mesopotamia and the palm was prolific in the south. Hourani has emphasised that a boat (planking, fastenings, sails and rigging) may be built from the palm tree and its fruit. Furthermore, a text of *c.* 2370 BC from the temple at Ban notes that ten different types of tree grew locally, two of them being specifically recommended for boatbuilding. On the other hand, there is evidence that, at least from the mid third millennium BC, Mesopotamia made up for a natural deficiency by importing highly desirable cedar logs from Lebanon.

Of the vessels depicted in de Graeve, the larger ones, and those with rams or other projections such as figureheads, or with more than one deck (i.e. biremes), probably represent planked vessels. Some of these are specifically identified as Phoenician in the text and others were probably also Phoenician since they had a particular shape of oar or sweep, or had a *hippos* figurehead.

**WATER TRANSPORT IN THE 1ST AND 2ND MILLENNIUM AD**
Sewn-plank boats
Sewn-plank boats have a long history in Arabia. Remains recently excavated in Oman and dated 2500 to 2200 BC, came from such boats waterproofed with bitumen (see p.26). Moreover, in chapter 36 of the first century AD *Periplus of the Erythraean Sea,* we learn that sewn-plank boats, known as *madarate*, were built in the vicinity of Omana (in Persis on the Makran coast, east of the Persian Gulf) and exported to Arabia (west of that gulf). Since Omana imported teak, *sissoo* and ebony from Barygaza in north-west India, it may be that those sewn-plank boats were built of such timbers.

In the sixth century AD Procopius noted that sewn boats were used in the Persian Gulf and, in the tenth century, Abu Zayd described how the bottoms of the sewn boats of Siragf on the River Tigris, were payed with oil mixed with other substances – probably dammar resin and lime, as used today. The oil, from whales caught in the Indian Ocean, not only filled the sewing holes but also protected the boat's timber from the teredo shipworm. In the twelfth century, Ibn Jubayr described the sewing process in more detail. Rush and grass bundles were bound together by palm fibre string and placed along the plank seams as caulking: the planking was then sewn together by coir cord made from coconut husk. Marco Polo noted that, in his day, treenails were used in the plank-fastening process: they were probably placed within the thickness of the planking to position the planks before sewing them together – as done in recent Arab sewn boats.

Amongst medieval European travellers who criticized Arab sewn plank boats, John of Montecorvino declared that they were 'frail and uncouth'. Others noted that they were 'badly built' and leaked badly and the crew were almost always bailing. Apart from Australia, there is worldwide evidence for the early use of sewn fastenings in plank boats. Moreover, it is a proven method of fastening the planking of seagoing vessels: sewn boats perform better than nailed boats on open coasts since their fastenings are resilient and they ride through heavy surf and readily withstand the shock of being beached. That criticism of Arab sewn boats was probably provoked by unfamiliarity, rather than being an objective appraisal.

A ninth century AD wreck with sewn planking and lashed-in frames and crossbeams was first investigated in 1998, in Indonesian waters off the island of Belitung. Initially, it was thought that this vessel might be the remains of an Indian ship, but recent timber species identification have shown that the cross beams were of teak (from India), the ceiling planking was from a region stretching from eastern Africa to the south west of the Arabian peninsula, while the remaining structural members (posts, frames, planking, and keelson) were from Africa. Using this information, the excavator concluded that this vessel had been built in the Middle East, perhaps in Oman or Yemen,

The shift from sewn to nailed fastenings
The advantages of nailed fastenings may not have become clear to Arabs until the late fifteenth century, when Portuguese three-masted, frame-first ships sailed into the Indian Ocean. Since these ships were built framing-first they did not have plank-to-plank fastenings, but nails were used to fasten planking to the already-erected framework. It is possible, however, that boats onboard those European ships continued to be built plank-first and thus had plank fastenings which became the stimulus for the change that seems to have taken place in Arab shipbuilding technology in the early sixteenth century. This was not a complete change since sewn-plank building survives today in Oman and Yemen.

James Hornell believed that Arab vessels of his day were built frame-first, but much evidence shows that, in fact, early twentieth century Arab sewn boats continued to be built plank-first. It thus seems likely that, in common with (almost?) all regions of the world, early Arab boats were also built plank-first. Again like much of the world,

Arabia continued to use this plank-first sequence into the post-medieval world.

The Hariri ship.(Fig.2.6)
In the AD 1237 manuscript known as al-Hariri's *Māqāmat*, is an illustration of an Arab ship – a two-masted, double-ended vessel with high, near-vertical, ends in which there are *oculi*. Her flush-laid planking is fastened together by intermittent paired stitches. A bowsprit

2.6. *An illustration from the 13ᵗʰ century manuscript al-Hariri's Māqāmat. (Bibliothéque nationale de France)*

projects forward of the bow and from it a grapnel anchor is catted. Below the weather deck there are two other decks, from the lower of which, two men are bailing out water. On the higher of the two internal decks are merchants, probably in cabins. Six of the crew are on the weather deck, steering or handling rigging, or are on lookout in the 'crow's nest'.

The dominating figure in this illustration is the helmsman who not only steers the vessel but also holds two lines of a sail set on the foremast. The helmsman is probably also the master since he holds a 'baton of authority' in his right hand – as does the master of a vessel depicted on one of the 2000 BC seals excavated from Bahrain. The Hariri master, in his helmsman's role, uses a median rudder held to the stern post by three pintles within gudgeons. Muir pointed out, long ago, that a later version of this Hariri ship, now in the Austrian National Library, is steered by a steering oar pivoted near the sternpost: this suggests that the thirteenth and fourteenth centuries were a time of change in Arab ships, including a shift to the median rudder.

Propulsion by Sail

In the first century AD, Strabo reported that Mesopotamian sails were similar to rush mats or wickerwork, an observation echoed by John of Montecorvino in the thirteenth century. The lines held by the master of the Hariri ship appear to be made fast to one edge and to an upper corner of a sail of indeterminate shape. In the recent past, Arab ships have been noted for their use of the lateen sail, notably the so-called 'Arab' settee-lateen (a quadrilateral sail with a short luff). Such sails were used in the eastern Mediterranean from the second century AD, and the triangular lateen from the fourth century AD. Depictions of Mesopotamian sailing ships on two 2000 BC stamp seals from Failaka, have a square sail set on a mast near amidships and there is no representation of a lateen sail in the Indian Ocean until centuries later: this suggests that the square sail may well have been the norm in the Arab world until medieval times.

Ibn Mājid (see p.39, 43) describes sails that, although four-sided, cannot have been rectangular in shape and thus could not have been square sails. Moreover his description of going about seems to be applicable to wearing rather than tacking. 'Wearing' involves passing the ship's stern, rather than her bows, through the wind and is almost invariably used by lateen-rigged vessels. Ibn Mājid also claimed that, in certain conditions, Arab vessels could be sailed within four points (*c.* 45°) of the relative wind. Such considerations suggest that by the fifteenth century Arabian ships set a fore-and-aft sail such as a lateen (Fig.2.7).

*2.7. Tim Severin's reconstruction sewn-plank boat, Sohar with a lateen main sail, off Malaca.*

## SEAFARING & NAVIGATION

As in Egypt, the necessity to forecast the seasonable flood of the Tigris and Euphrates, led to astronomy, mathematics and a calendar: this was followed by land and sea navigation using the stars. The Persians were early overseas navigators, aware of the fixed direction of the pole and using the rising and setting of selected stars as the basis of a direction system. A Persian collection of sailing directions was subsequently used by Arabs. As Islam expanded, it became necessary to describe land and sea routes and the position of newly encountered lands. This led to a rapid increase in the practice of navigation based on translations of Persian, Indian and Greek works into Arabic.

Observatories were established at Baghdad, Damascus, Cairo, Samarkand, Toledo, and Cordova and, by the tenth century, Arabs were regularly sailing to all parts of the Indian Ocean, to Jidda in the Red Sea and along the east African coast as far south as Sofola at 20° S. Arab seamen also sailed the Mediterranean and may have ventured into the Atlantic as early as the tenth century. Arab merchants were established in Sri Lanka by AD 414 and, by the mid eighth century, there were regular sailings to China. Tim Severin's passage (Fig. 2.7) in 1982 from Oman to Canton was partly inspired by Ibn Wahab's *Voyage of Sulayman the Merchant,* published in *c.* AD 850, which contained useful information about tides, typhoons, landmarks and sources of fresh water.

The fifteenth century Arab navigator, Ibn Mājid al-Najdi, recognised that different styles of navigation were required on three distinctive types of passage:

- Coastal. Pilotage techniques were used.
- Direct routes. On a direct passage across the sea between two points the altitude of the pole star (latitude) was taken on departure from the first port, and also on making a landfall on the far side. During such passages dead reckoning methods were used: a known course in *rhumbs* (compass points) was steered and the distance run was estimated (in *isba* – a measure of change of latitude).
- Indirect routes. On a passage out of sight of land, involving a change of course, a form of 'latitude sailing' was used. A given course (generally north/south) was steered until the 'latitude' of the destination (by observations of star altitude) was reached. Course was then altered direct for the destination, maintaining that 'star altitude'.

## Pilotage in coastal waters

A pilot's duties are described in some pre-Islamic literature similar to the Sanskrit text *Jatakamata* that was translated into Chinese before the mid fifth century. "A pilot must recognise the distant approach of good and bad weather, and identify different regions by the fish and birds seen there, by the mountains and other landmarks, by the colour of the water and by the nature of the bottom (using lead and line)". By the twelfth century, the unit *gama* (a fathom, from finger tip to finger tip of outstretched arms) was used to measure depths of water.

In his fifteenth century navigational 'manuals', Ibn Mājid noted soundings and the nature of the bottom in coastal waters and in the approaches to harbours over much of the world then known to Arabs. He also documented reefs and shoals in the Red Sea and off the east coast of Africa, and drew attention to landmarks such as atolls and mountain peaks. Ibn Mājid identified the four principal problems that a pilot could face in inshore waters: inaccurate estimates of tidal drift and leeway; a compass defect; a dozing helmsman; and an inability to take accurate star altitudes.

## Navigation out of sight of land

The prospect of increasing overseas trade seems to have stimulated Arabian pilots to find improved navigational techniques. As a result of these advances in navigation, there was a spectacular increase in Arab economic growth. The simultaneous increase in astronomical knowledge provided Arab seamen with the tabulated data needed to consolidate their seagoing experience.

### *Directions and courses*

As in all maritime cultures, early Arab navigators based relative directions on the boat's heading, using such terms as 'ahead', 'windward bow' and 'on the beam'. For absolute directions they used a system based on the celestial pole (the null point about which the heavens apparently rotate). In daytime, or at night when the sky was obscured, it is likely that they used systems based on other 'fixed points' such as the wind, the swell, and the sun at sunrise, noon and sunset. Generally, Arab seafaring was undertaken in relatively low latitudes (*c.* 10° N to 25° S) in which the heavens appear to rotate at a less-oblique angle than in higher latitudes: thus the sun gives a more accurate indication of east and west.

Using one of these 'fixed points' as a datum, the horizon can be divided into points or *rhumbs*. With the celestial pole as a fixed point ('north') and facing that way, 'south' is at your back, 'west' on your left hand and 'east' on your right hand: that is the essence of a 'star compass'. Points midway between the four cardinals can then be recognised and named 'north-east', 'south–east' and so on. This sub-division can continue until one arrives at thirty-two points, each one indicating an arc of 11¼°. Such points were additionally identified with the rising and setting of specific stars or constellations: ENE was the direction on which Arcturus rose, and WNW on which it set. Ibn Mājid further divided his 'star rose' to make 224 *isba* ('fingers'), each one equivalent to 1° 37′ in azimuth. In pre-Islamic times, Persians had identified predominant winds with particular points. Ibn Mājid also used that system: the north-east monsoon wind came from 'the East, but a little towards the North'; the south-west wind came from 'between the rhumb of Canopus setting [SSW] and West'. Similar systems linking celestial bodies and recognizable winds (a 'wind compass') evolved in the pre-Classical Mediterranean, in Viking Age north-west Europe, and doubtless elsewhere.

The Chinese are thought to have known the directional properties of the lodestone by the first century AD, but the earliest documented use of a magnetised needle at sea seems to have been towards the end of the eleventh century when it was used by Persian and Arab ships on passages between India, Sumatra and Canton. This magnetic compass was more an auxiliary aid, to be used in overcast weather, rather than a primary means of navigation. Whenever possible, the mariner continued to conn his ship by reference to the natural elements.

*Distance measurement*
The *isba* was not only a unit of angular measure, it was also used

linearly to derive a measure of distance in the north-south direction i.e. change of latitude. If, between two readings, the altitude (angular elevation) of the Pole changed by one *isbâ*, the change in latitude was one *tirfa* (equivalent to 96 nm). Arab navigators adopted the *zam*, an Indian unit for measuring distances unrelated to latitude. This *zam* (equivalent to ⅛ *isba* = 12 nm) was the distance sailed in one watch (three hours): a 'day's sail' would thus be ninety-six miles. A day's sail due north would increase the altitude of Polaris by one *isbā*. Another unit was the *farsakh* which appears to have been the equivalent of the European 'league' that is, "the standard distance sailed in one hour" which was taken to be 3 nm.

## *Measurement of Latitude*
Ibn Mājid gives latitude in terms of star altitude (angular elevation) for many places in those seas usually sailed by Arabs. At first such altitudes were measured in hand breadths, the hand being held at arm's length. Al Khwarizmi designed a staff for measuring such altitudes in the ninth century, and by the end of that century wooden tablets were used: these appear to have been the forerunner of the *kamal* which consisted of tablets of different sizes thus catering for a range of

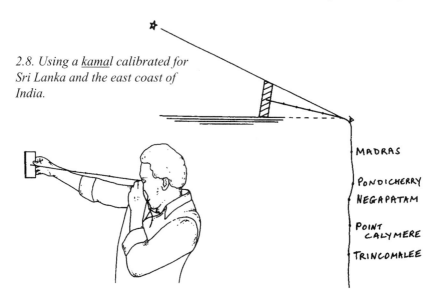

2.8. *Using a kamal calibrated for Sri Lanka and the east coast of India.*

MADRAS

PONDICHERRY

NEGAPATAM

POINT CALYMERE

TRINCOMALEE

angles. A string on which knots had been tied at graduated intervals was fastened to the centre of each tablet which was held at eye level by a navigator sitting down, and moved towards the target star until it apparently filled the gap between horizon and star (Fig.2.8). The length of string, indicated by the number of knots, measured the vertical angle in *isba* – the fewer the knots, the greater that angle.

Quadrants and astrolabes were also known to medieval Arab navigators. The first Arabic sea astrolabe, probably based on a Greek model, was made in AD 771; the quadrant was perfected in the tenth century

## *Landfall*

Ibn Mājid described some of the many signs that indicate approaching land and noted the coastal topography and oceanography of many places, especially on the west coast of India. Similar, but more limited, advice had been given in the first century AD *Periplus* (see p.75, 76).

## *Aids to navigation*

Arab 'charts' of the Indian Ocean from China to Africa were seen in AD 985 in the library of the Prince of Khurasan, but it is not clear whether they were usable or merely decorative. Towards the end of the fifteenth century Vasco da Gama undoubtedly saw seagoing charts onboard Arab ships, and he was very ready to use them. *Rahmani* (a 'rutter' or pilot's handbook') were available from the ninth or tenth century, and treatises on astronomy and astronomical tables were also first produced 600 years or so before Ibn Mājid, the navigator, produced his books and poems.

## Ibn Mājid

Ibn Mājid had more than fifty years' experience at sea when he produced his major works. His publications on navigation are masterly and, after due acknowledgement to God, he was not slow to praise his own skills. It seems very likely that he was the pilot who guided Vasco da Gama from Africa to India in 1488. His writings may be summarised under four heads:

- The training and duties of a ship's master.
- Details (including astronomical observations) of passages in the Red Sea, the Persian Gulf, the Indian Ocean and the Malay Archipelago.
- Data on coastal waters, including coastal profiles, currents, winds, tides and depths of water. The position of shoals, reefs and major landmarks.
- Latitudes of places; times and distances between places; and the correct method of dividing the horizon.

Harbours (Fig.2.9)

Arabian places mentioned in the first century AD *Periplus of the Erythraean Sea* as havens or trading stations, may be divided into three types:

*2.9. Map of the Red Sea & Persian Gulf region showing harbours.*

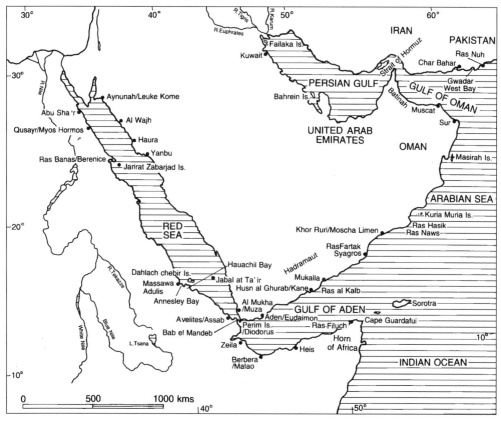

- Simple landing places with fresh water.
  Okêlis (Ch.7 & 25) on the east side of the strait. Bab el Mandeb, probably on a lagoon. By the time of Ptolemy, Okêlis had become an emporion.
- Regional Trading Places.
  Leukê Kômê (Ch. 19) A Nabataean trading place from where there was a route to Petra, the regional capital. It was probably where Khuraybah now stands.
  Sachalitês (Ch. 29 & 30) This Hadramaut coast trading place was in a deep bay protected by a fortress on a headland (probably Ras Fartak).
  Moscha Limên (Ch. 32). This was a designated harbour with a mole, more than 100 nautical miles west of Syagros (Ras Fartak). It is identified as Khor Ruri, an inlet west of Ras Naws.
- Entrepôt for International Trade.
  Eudaimôn Arabia (Ch. 26) The name translates as 'prosperous Arabia'- the harbour subsequently became known as Aden. This entrepôt, 100 n.m. to the east of Bab el Mandeb, was where cargo from and to India was transhipped. Westbound ships might have to wait there for a shift in wind to take them northwards through the Red Sea. It continued to prosper into medieval times: in the late thirteenth century, Marco Polo noted that much Indian merchandise went through the port.
  Muza (Ch. 7, 16, 17, 21, 24, 25, 31) This is identified as Mocha / al Mukha, *c.* 35 nm north of the strait Bab el Mandreb.
  Kanê (Ch. 27, 28). This is identified as Ouana, to the east of Cape Hasn al Ghurab, *c.* 200 nm east of Eudaimôn Arabia.
  Apologos (Ch. 35) in the Kingdom of Persis, at the head of the Persian Gulf. This was probably Basra on the Shatt al Arab.
  Omana (Ch. 36). Another port in Persis, *c.* 300 nm to the east of the Strait of Hormuz. Sewn plank boats were built here and exported to Arabia. This may be Chā Bāhar or Tiz on the Makran coast of Iran, or it may have been further east at Gwadar West Bay or Pasni in western Pakistan.

# CHAPTER 3

# India

This chapter deals with South Asia which includes Pakistan, Bangladesh and Sri Lanka, as well as India itself. The region extends in latitude from 30°–35°N, well north of the Tropic of Cancer, to near the Equator at *c.* 5°N; in longitude from *c.* 65° to *c.* 95° E. In effect, this sub-continent is a large peninsula bounded by the Arabian Sea to the west, the Bay of Bengal to the east and the Indian Ocean to the south. It is separated from the rest of Asia by the Hindu Kush, the Karakorum and the Himalayan mountain ranges to the north (Fig.3.1).

In northern India there are two great river systems: the Indus in the west and the Ganges-Brahmaputra in the east. Their enormous catchment areas collect water from a range of climatic regimes and the rivers have immense flood plains and very large deltas. In one main aspect they differ: in the Ganges-Brahmaputra system there is moderate to high rainfall, whereas the Indus (like the Nile and the Tigris-Euphrates), although having high rainfall in its upper reaches, flows through a desert in its lower reaches where there is virtually no rainfall. From early times until the coming of the railways, both river systems were not only the principal means of communications within their regions, but also gateways to the sea and overseas trade.

In peninsular India, there are other rivers of considerable size each one of which, within its individual region, is comparable with, but smaller than, the two great northern systems. The delta areas of three such east-coast rivers became the nuclei of Iron Age and later kingdoms: the River Kaveri in Tamil Nadu; Krishna-Godavari in Andhra Pradesh; and Mahanadi in Orissa.

The South Asian climate is generally tropical with seasonal

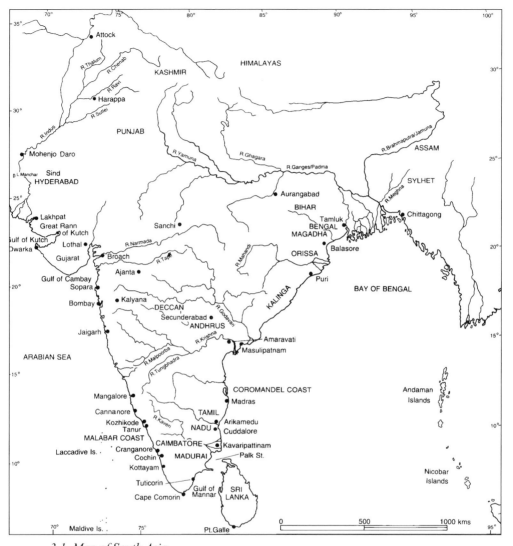

*3.1. Map of South Asia.*

monsoon winds having a profound effect on the coastal and overseas sailing seasons (Fig.3.2). On the west coast stormy, wet winds of the south-west monsoon prevent sailing from May to August, but from then until November it becomes practicable. December to March is the main sailing season with coastal vessels using the daily land and sea breezes, but from April it becomes increasingly more difficult to make such passages. The south-west monsoon has a less disturbing

47

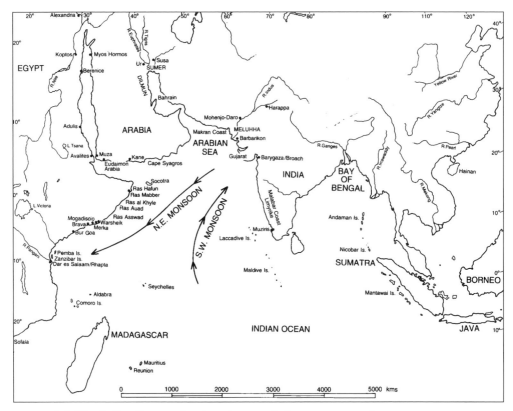

*3.2. The Indian Ocean, showing characteristic monsoon tracks.*

effect on the east coast: sailing can be undertaken from June to September, except during certain periods at the head of the Bay of Bengal. The north-east monsoon is more aggressive on this coast bringing sailing to a halt from October to December and sometimes later. From January until May there is usually good sailing with a north-west wind changing to regular land and sea breezes, then to south-east and south winds.

## EUROPEAN CONTACTS WITH INDIA

There is little Indian documentation of early trade between India and Europe, but Greek and Roman authors, and some excavated evidence, allow an outline description of the later stages of such contacts to be compiled. During the reign of Ptolemy II, ruler of Egypt from 146 to 117 BC, the Greek Eudoxus of Cyzicus sailed from Egypt to India, guided by an Indian pilot who had been shipwrecked in the Gulf of Aden. Strabo's (2.3.4) account (quoting Poseidonius) of this event seems to be the earliest record of a Mediterranean seaman using monsoon winds to cross the Arabian Sea. After the Roman conquest of Egypt in 30 BC, use of this trade route significantly increased: Strabo (2.5.12) noted that, in his day, 120 ships left *Myos Hormus* (near Kosseir/Qusayt) for India each year whereas, in earlier times, only a few had attempted such passages. These trading voyages continued until the fifth, possibly sixth, century AD.

Those ships (probably of the Mediterranean tradition, but built in the Red Sea region) returned to one of two harbours on the western coast of the Red Sea: *Berenice* (in Foul Bay, south of Ras Banas) or (occasionally) Myos Hormus. There they were met by Alexandrian merchants who had sailed up the River Nile as far as Coptos, then trekked along the desert road through the Wadi Hammamat, eastwards to the Red Sea coast (Fig.1.10). It is not clear how much Indian shipping (if any) was involved in this trade, but Strabo (2.3.4) noted that, before his time, Indian ships had traded with the Persian Gulf region.

From the seventh to the twelfth century AD, east-west trade in the Indian Ocean seems to have been entirely undertaken by Arabs. From the thirteenth century onwards, glimpses of India were given by European travellers such as Marco Polo (who also visited the Andoman and Nicobar islands), and the early fifteenth century Franciscan, Odoric of Pordenone, who sailed from the Persian Gulf to India where he visited the Malabar coast and Sri Lanka.

Between 1432 and 1485, Portuguese seamen made progress southwards along the West African coast by first sailing out into the southern Atlantic. In 1488 Bartholemeu Diaz rounded the southern tip of Africa and sailed eastwards, beyond Cape Elizabeth. In 1497, Vasco da Gama rounded the Cape of Good Hope and sailed eastwards then northwards into the Indian Ocean. After calling at several harbours along the African east coast, da Gama came to Malindi in Kenya. He sailed from there on 24 April 1498 with an Arab pilot, probably Ibn Mājid of Gujarat, and, after a twenty-three day passage across the Arabian Sea, made a landfall on the Western Ghats, subsequently anchoring off Calicot (Kozhikode). When da Gama left the Malabar coast at the end of August he had to tack against the south-west monsoon wind and took four months to make the African coast. From this time onwards European trade with India grew, and with such contacts came increasing knowledge of the boats of the sub-continent.

## WATER TRANSPORT
### Excavated boats
There have been very few finds of Indian water transport – a ninth century AD vessel wrecked off the Indonesian island of Belitung, between Sumatra and Borneo, which  was first thought might be Indian, is now considered to be Arabian (see p.35).  The few finds that have been published are late in date: a sixth to fourth century BC logboat from the Kelani Ganga in the Colombo district of Sri Lanka; a sixteenth century AD barge-like vessel – possibly of European design – in an abandoned tributary of the River Boro Bulong near Balasore in Orissa; and a boat dated by radiocarbon to AD $80 \pm 40$ from the River Gumani on the west bank of the Ganges, some 250 km north of Calcutta. Boat remains at Kadakkarappally on the Malabar coast of the Indian south-west state of Kerala, excavated in 2002–3, proved to be parts of a well-preserved, double-planked hull of a flat-bottomed boat, some 20 m in length. The hull, built from locally-grown timber, was divided into eleven compartments by ten floor timbers with slots into which bulkheads had been inserted. Iron spikes and wooden treenails were found and both inner and outer planking appear to have been fastened together by nails clenched over a rove. There were two mast steps: one near amidships; the second towards the bow. Radiocarbon determinations suggest a date in the range thirteenth to fifteenth centuries AD. Like the 'barge-like vessel' excavated from Olandazsahi on the river Boro Bulong in Orissa, this boat was probably from the sixteenth or seventeenth century when European techniques were first influencing Indian boatbuilding traditions.

Early representational and documentary evidence

During the early third millennium BC a Bronze Age culture, now known as 'Harappan', developed along the valley of the lower Indus and on the Gujarat coast. During the 1,500 or so years that this river-based culture lasted, overseas trade was established with Egypt and Mesopotamia. In the late third millennium BC, Sargon of Agade in Mesopotamia inscribed steles and statues proclaiming, among other matters, that ships from Meluhha (? the River Indus region) came to the harbour near his capital city.

Five clay models of boats excavated from Lothal, an Harappan site near the head of the Gulf of Cambay, probably represent flat-bottomed, plank boats, but structural details are unclear. A graffito on a *c.* 2000 BC, Harappan potsherd from Mohenjo-Daro, on the central stretch of the River Indus, is an 'outline sketch' of a planked boat with a steering oar on the quarter and a mast stepped near amidships: this is the earliest evidence for sail in India. (Fig.3.3). An impression on a seal and another on a baked clay amulet, both from Mohenjo-Daro, probably depict river bundle rafts with two steering oars at the stern and superstructure amidships.

*3.3. Graffito of a masted boat on a potsherd of c. 2000 BC from Mohenjo-daro: the earliest Indian evidence for sail.*

Masted vessels are depicted in outline on second/first century BC coins from Chandraketugarj in the Ganges delta and similar vessels are shown on a Sri Lankan monument and on first century BC terracotta seals. Boats, with planking fitted together with joggles and projections (as seen, in much earlier times, on the Cheops ship (see p.7–10), and fastened by flat, double-dovetail shaped clamps, are depicted on a second century BC medallion from a monastery at Baharhut, and on the east gate of a first century BC Stupa 1 at Sanchi in central India (Fig.3.4). Two-masted ships, with a sheerline rising towards bow and stern, are seen on coins found along the Andhra, Bay of Bengal coast that had been issued by the second century AD Satavanhanas. These vessels have a steering oar on each quarter and their shroud-less masts are supported by forestay and backstay. There is also a ship symbol depicted on coins found on the Coromandel coast that were probably issued by the Pallavas in the fourth century AD.

*3.4. Boat with double-dovetailed plank fastenings, depicted on a 1st century BC stupa at Sanchi.*

These Bay of Bengal coastal finds, together with other evidence, suggest that, by the second to fourth century AD, settlements under Satavanhana rule, in the lower reaches of the Rivers Krishna and Godavari, were involved in overseas trade. Ships are also depicted in the fourth to sixth century AD Buddhist sites at Ajanta (in western India) and in Aurangabad (in the Ganges river system). The vessel depicted in a cave at the latter site has two (possible three) masts, each fitted with stays. A vessel with *oculi* at both ends, depicted in Cave 1 at Ajanta, has hulc-like planking, a feature found nowadays in boats built in Bangladesh, Bengal and Orissa.

Floats and rafts
Inflated skins used as personal floats are depicted on the first century BC Stupa at Sanchi. Since such floats (and almost every other known-type of float) are used in India today, they were probably used from early prehistoric times. Rafts of light timbers, given extra buoyancy by inflated hide floats (Fig.3.5) or by sealed pots, have also been used in recent times. Float rafts are nowadays mainly found in the upper reaches of the Indus and the Ganges, and in Kashmir and the Punjab. The earliest reference to them is in the *Memoirs* of Emperor Jahangir who reigned from 1605 to 1627. Pot rafts ('chatty rafts') are mostly used in the lower reaches of rivers south of the Punjab and the Himalayas foothills: they were first described in the seventeenth century by the Venetian, Niccolao Manucci.

Log rafts are first mentioned in Ch. 60 of the first century AD *Periplus of the Erythraean Sea*: the *sangara* is said to be a seagoing raft of the Coromandel coast. South Indian log rafts were subsequently noted by Balbi and Fryer in the sixteenth century. A more detailed account was given in the seventeenth century by Thomas Bowrey who noted that the *catamaran* had four, five or six logs lashed together, with the central log(s) being longer than the others, giving this raft its distinctive shape (Fig.3.6). Such rafts were propelled by paddles: the larger ones carried three to five tons of cargo; the smaller were used for fishing. In the mid nineteenth century, Thomas Edye, chief shipwright in the naval dockyard at Trincomalee in Sri Lanka, reported

*3.5. A mid-20th century buoyed raft on the River Swat, northern Pakistan.*

that catamaran logs were connected together by three spreaders lashed to the logs through small holes. Catamarans were usually propelled by paddle, but in monsoon weather they were fitted with an outrigger and a sail. Boat-shaped, log rafts, under sail, are much used today for fishing in the coastal waters off India's Bay of Bengal coast, from Orissa southwards to Cape Comorin and the southern parts of Travancore, and along the northern shores of Sri Lanka. In Tamil Nadu, log rafts, known as *kattu maram* (logs bound), are used to catch flying fish. Two large *guares* fins are fitted between the logs of these rafts to reduce leeway and assist in sailing balance (see p.94–5, 109–111, 165–166).

Bundle rafts are depicted on an Harappan seal and a baked clay amulet from Mohenjo-Daro: both are dated to the Indus civilisation, 2500–1500 BC. They have a steering oar pivoted on one quarter and superstructure amidships. Fifteen hundred years or so later, Herodotus

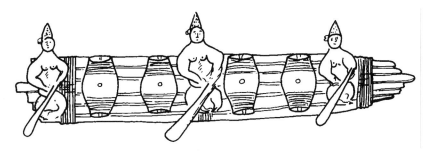

*3.6. A 17ᵗʰ century catamaran (log raft) drawn by Thomas Bowrey.*

(3.98) reported that such craft were used for fishing on Indian rivers. In the first century AD, Pliny (*NH*.24.82) described how vessels made of reeds, with rigging similar to that of Nile boats, sailed from the River Ganges to Sri Lanka in twenty days. As there is no tradition of waterproofing bundles of reed in India (unlike Arabia), these vessels were probably rafts, rather than boats. It seems likely that, at intervals during those twenty days (possibly nightly), they were beached to allow the reeds to dry. Reed bundle rafts were still being used on Indian rivers and lakes in the twentieth century.

Hide Boats
The hide boats of southern India are made from readily available materials: bamboo, hide and coir, with tar as a paying and seam-sealer. The boat's circular form is the simplest way of making a basketry framework (Figs 3.7, 3.8, 3.9); moreover such boats can be steered and propelled from any position, the paddler sitting or squatting, facing forward in the leading part of the boat. India's hide boats are not (and may never have been) used at sea, but on rivers and lakes. They are very suited to the fast-flowing, rock-strewn headwaters of southern Indian rivers which, within a single day, can vary greatly in their course, depth and flow. The hide boat's lightweight, yet resilient, structure allows it to be used in shallow water and to transport relatively great loads, yet, when empty, it can be carried by one man. Simplicity, cheapness and fitness for purpose are the characteristics of this boat.

*3.7. The framework
of a Tamil Nadu hide
boat nearing
completion.*

*3.8. The interior of a
completed hide boat.*

*3.9. Hide boats
after use.*

The earliest known reference to hide boats is from 1398 when they were said to have been used to ferry troops across the River Krishna in Andhra Pradesh. There are three, early sixteenth century, stone inscriptions in Karnatika referring to hide boats (*harigolu*) on the River Tungabhadra. Three hundred years later, large, circular hide boats, 10–20 ft (3–6 m) in diameter, were used as ferries and for fishing in Hyderabad/Secunderabad in Andhra: these boats were of ox-hide on a basketry framework and were propelled by two paddlers. Until the late twentieth century, similar boats were used in the higher reaches of the rivers of Andhra Pradesh, Karnataka and Tamil Nadu. Such boats were bowl or saucer-shaped and varied in size from one-man fishing boats, 1.5 to 1.8 m diameter, to boats 4.2 m in diameter, able to carry 30 to 50 men or 4 tonnes of rice. The 'skin' of such boats was made of ox hides (2½ hides for a medium-sized boat) stitched together, then fastened to an open basketry framework of split bamboo by lashings just below the rim (gunwale) of the framework where it had been re-enforced by a stout bundle of bamboos. The primary framework of such boats was reinforced by secondary, sometimes tertiary, framing.

In the late-1980s/early 1990s, hides were generally replaced by two layers of plastic (ex fertiliser) bags sewn together. Around that time also, the framework of the 2–3 m diameter boats at Hogenakal, on the headwaters of the River Kaveri in Tamil Nadu, seems to have been simplified by omitting the tertiary framework and by reducing the number of bamboos in the secondary layer but fastening together, at the interstices, those remaining. These changes were probably the result of a shift in the main role of these boats from transporting animals and goods, to carrying tourists.

### Pottery Boats

Tigari or gamla are large earthenware basins, hemispherical in shape, and some 2½ ft (0.8 m) in diameter, with a reinforced rim, recently used in Bangladesh by one person to cross steams or flooded fields, and occasionally for fishing. Similar pot boats are used in China . Two thousand years ago, Strabo (17.1.4) noted their use as ferries in the Nile delta.

Logboats

A logboat, found in the River Kelani in 1952 and now in Sri Lanka's National Museum in Colombo, was recently dated by radiocarbon to the sixth to fourth century BC. There are several paired holes through its upper sides, *c.* 1.10 m apart, where an outrigger may once have been fitted. Pliny (*NH* 6.26.105) tells us that, in his day, logboats brought pepper from the Indian District of Cottonara downstream to the harbour at Pirakad on the Malabar coast. In the early seventeenth century, Linschoten depicted what appear to be two seagoing, double-ended logboats: one a *palegua*, propelled by two oarsmen and steered by a third; the other a *tomes* being poled, with a roofed 'cabin' amidships.

In the early nineteenth century Edye reported that Malabar logboats, made from a single log, measured 8 to 20 x 1.5 to 2.0 x 1.0 to 1.5 ft. They were propelled by paddle and used for river fishing and cargo-carrying. Other logboats documented by Edye appear to have been extended by the addition of a high curving stern and drooping bow, and possibly a capping to the sides. The largest of these Cochin 'snake boats', measuring 60 x 3 ft (18 x 1 m) and, manned by twenty paddlers, are said to have made 11 knots. Particular trees, of above average length (to give speed) and breadth (to house double-banked paddlers), must have been chosen for these boats. The Cochin *bandar manché* logboat, extended on each side by a sewn strake, carried up to 18 tons of cargo to and from ships anchored in Cochin roads. Edye noted that 'ribs' were spaced at about 5 ft (1.5 m) across the bottom of these boats: these were probably ridges worked in the solid log that either marked the stations for each paddler or on which cargo was loaded to keep it clear of bilge water.

The Point de Galle 'canoe' was another logboat extended by sewn washstrakes, but this one also had a single outrigger and her mast was fastened to the forward of the outrigger's two booms. Edye does not describe the sail, but as the mast was stepped well forward, it may have been a lugsail, as was fitted to Point de Gallé 'canoes' used in the strait between India and Sri Lanka in the early twentieth century.

Two simple, early nineteenth century, Malabar logboats were joined side-by-side to form a pair known as a *jangār*: in this manner greater stability and increased cargo space were obtained. Such boats were used to ferry cattle, horses, baggage and carts and other bulky articles. In the twentieth century, these pairs were known as *jangada*, *jangadam* or *sangadam*. Logboat stability can also be increased by expanding a basic logboat so that its waterline beam measurement becomes significantly greater, thus converting a river boat into one that could be used in an estuary or even at sea. In recent times at Tinnevelly in Tamil Nadu, after a specially selected log had been hollowed, it was made malleable by filling it with water heated by hot stones or by the sun. The sides were then forced apart, ribs inserted to hold that shape, and washstrakes added to regain height of sides. Wherever logboats are expanded today, or are known to have been so treated in the recent past, it seems likely that the technique was used there in earlier times, possibly as early as the Bronze Age.

Sewn Plank Boats

Although the sewn plank boats of Arabia and east Africa are mentioned in the *Periplus*, such boats are not mentioned in the Indian chapters. The earliest traceable reference to Indian sewn boats is by Duarte Barbosa, a Portuguese who worked on the Malabar coast from 1500 to 1515. He stated that, annually in February, such boats sailed from Calicot, on the Malabar coast, to the Red Sea, some going to Aden and some to Jeddah (for Mecca): the return passage was between August and October. These sewn plank vessels were of some 200 tonnes and they had 'keels like the Portuguese'. Barbosa also noted that sewn-plank boats were built from palm tree timber in the Maldives island.

At about the same time, Gasparo Balbi described boats of the Coromandel coast that were 'sown with fine cords': these oared boats took passengers and merchandise from ships through heavy surf to the shore (Fig.3.10). Thomas Bowrey – late seventeenth century pepper trader, gave more details about the sewn boats of India's east coast (generally known as '*masula*').These were flat-bottomed boats with broad, thin planks sewn with *cayre* (coir), that had crossbeams/thwarts, but no other framing timbers. They were used through the

*3.10 An early-19<sup>th</sup> century sewn-plank boat on the Coromandel foreshore. (Admiral Pâris)*

surf, carrying bales of calico or silk: their flexible structure was 'most proper for this coast'. A near contemporary, Dr Fryer, noted that *masula* planking was fastened together with rope yarn of the *cocoe*: the joints were then caulked with *dammar* – a tree gum or resin.

In the early nineteenth century, Edye published drawings and descriptions of five types of sewn boats – two from Coromandel, and three from Malabar. Edye's Madras *masula* was generally similar in form and structure to Bowrey's seventeenth century boat: these frameless craft measured 30-35 x 10-11 x 7-8 ft (9-11 x 3 x 2m) and were sewn with coir yarn over wadding. They were steered by an oar over each quarter, and propelled by twelve men, two to each thwart, with bamboo oars. Time was kept by the steersman varying the rhythm of a song to match the surf's wave pattern. Echoing Fryer, Edye emphasised that *masulas* were intentionally built with a pliable structure so that they would absorb the shock experienced when taking the ground: unsurprisingly, two of the crew were employed bailing-out water.

By Edye's time, other types of Indian sewn boat had been influenced by Arab boatbuilding techniques. The Panyani *manché*, a

Coromandel coastal vessel, was framed and had a raked mast; the three types of the Malabar coast had also been changed: the Mangalore *manché*, a poled, river cargo boat, retained the general hull shape of the *masula*, but its stern was adapted to take a rudder; the Calicot *manché* adopted a raking Arab-style bow; and, while the smaller *patamar* remained sewn, the larger ones were 'bolted and nailed in the European fashion'. Furthermore, both large and small *patāmar* adopted the hull shape of contemporary Arab dows.

Admiral Pâris' detailed drawing of a Malabar *patāmar* with a long, overhanging bow (also seen in Edye's drawing) shows that the strake edges were interlocked in a N-shaped rabbet (an angular form of the half-lap joint) with a metal spike driven from inboard, at an angle through the seam into the lower strake. The strakes were also fastened by lashings tightened by wooden wedges. Stavorinus, who visited the Gujarat coast in the late eighteenth century, recorded that this fastening technique was known as *vadhera*. The rabbet was lined with a cotton strip and resin; the two strakes were then laced together at 5 ft (1.5 m) intervals in a diagonal manner through two holes in each strake- a thin wedge was then driven into each lashing on the inboard side. The strakes were then further fastened together by spikes (*vadhera*-fashion) at 200mm intervals. The spikes were spaced relatively closely but, by themselves, could not keep the seams closed, and, since the lashings were the first fastenings, this *patāmar* may be considered a sewn boat.

At the beginning of the twentieth century, Wilson noted that frames were fastened to the *patāmar*'s planking by large nails clenched by turning their points along the inner face of the frames. In the 1920s Hornell noted no lashings in Gujaret boats, but reported that, after the strake seams had been spiked, the 'planks were spiked down to the frames' that had been 'first set up in the ordinary manner'. Thus, by that date, Gujaret boats were built frame-first. Nevertheless, the planking was still fastened together by nails, *vadhera* fashion, although it was no longer sewn or lashed.

One of the tenth to thirteenth century stone carvings recently discovered in northern Goa depicts a sewn plank boat: similar boats are used today on the rivers of northern Goa to transport sand.

Moreover, the twenty-first century *masula* or *chelingue* of the Coromandel coast is similar in form and in structure to those described by Bowrey, Edye and Pâris. In 1973 there were 4,700 frameless, sewn-plank boats on the east coast of India between Cape Comorin in the south and Paradeep in Orissa. Indian sewn-plank boats can be traced back only as far as that medieval stone carving and those early sixteenth century accounts. Since sewn-plank boats are known to have been used during the late first millennium BC/early first millennium AD in east Africa, Arabia and South-East Asia, there has almost certainly been similar early use in India.

Other plank fastenings
Three other Indian fastenings remain to be mentioned. Two of these were first noted in the early nineteenth century; the earliest evidence for the third is from the eleventh to twelfth century, but its use in India was not documented until the late eighteenth century, and its importance was not recognised until the mid-1950s.

*Spikes as edge-to-edge fastenings*
In the early nineteenth century, Admiral Paris noted that, on the Malabar coast, boats with flush-laid planking (edge-to-edge or half-lap) had notches cut at intervals along the lower edge of each strake into which spikes were driven obliquely, across the seam, into the plank below. Similar plank fastenings were used on boats of the Gujarat coast and on the large, seagoing sampans of Chittagong in Bangladesh.

*Treenails*
Boats known as Calcuttan *manchés* of the Malabar coast, and the *punt* and the *bohatja* of the Indus valley, were fastened by treenails driven obliquely through the edges of flush-laid planking.

*Reverse-clinker planking and hulc planking patterns*
Reverse-clinker planking boats are built with each succeeding strake overlapping inboard the upper edge of the strake below, rather than

outboard as in European clinker (Fig.3.11). The earliest known depictions are on three, eleventh- to twelfth- century monumental carvings: one is in the walls of the Jagamohana temple in Puri; the others are in the Indian Museum, Calcutta (Fig.3.12) and in the Victoria and Albert Museum in London. In the late eighteenth century, the Belgian artist, Solvyns depicted a *"pettoo-a* from Balasore" with reverse-clinker planking (Fig.3.13), and his *"pataily* of Behar and Benares" probably also has that feature. Boats built with reverse-clinker planking were first recorded in the 1950s by Dr Basil Greenhill in Sylhet, Bangladesh. In 1997–8, a boat type (*patia*), with similar planking, was documented along the Bay of Bengal coast from the Rivers Boro Bulong and Subarnarekha in northern Orissa, north-eastward towards the Bengal River systems (Figs 3.14 & 3.15).

*3.11. European clinker and Indian reverse-clinker.*

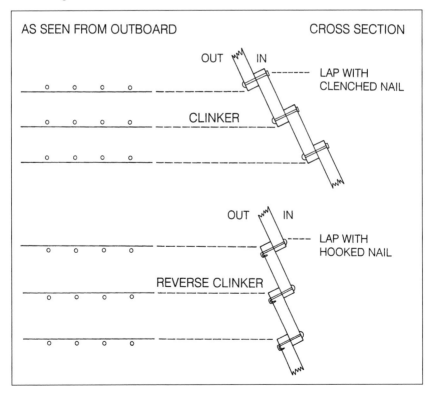

*3.12. An 11th/12th century stone relief from Orissa depicting a boat with reverse-clinker planking (Indian Museum, Calcutta).*

*3.13. A late-18th century drawing by F.B.Solvyns of a pettoo-a 'from Balasore or the coast of Palmira'.*

*3.14. Inside the unfinished bow of a patia at Talesari in northern Orissa. The ends of each strake of reverse-clinker planking are broadened to provide a landing for the next higher strake.*

*3.15. The bows of an oared patia at Digha in southern West Bengal. Her reverse-clinker planking is laid 'hulc fashion', rising at the ends to finish on an angled line. Strakes laid in European clinker fashion 'fill the gap' between the two ends.*

*3.16. Reverse-clinker boats being used to extract and transport stone on the River Pijain at Bolla Ghat, Sylhet district, Bangladesh, in 1997. In the foreground are graded piles of boulders, stones and shingle.*

In northern Bangladesh small, reverse-clinker boats are widely used on rivers when levels are low to extract stone brought downstream from the Himalayas during the flood season (Fig.3.16). The reverse-clinker strakes of these boats are fastened together by staples driven from outboard at intervals along the upper edge of the lower plank, and by other staples driven from inboard alongside the lower edge of the upper plank. These staples are clenched by hooking the emergent points back into the planking. In Orissa and west Bengal, nails are driven from inboard (rather than outboard as in western Europe clinker planking) through the overlap of the *patia*'s reverse-clinker strakes and are clenched outboard by hooking the point of the nail back into lower plank.

Another characteristic of the reverse-clinker boats of India and Bangladesh is that their lower planking does not end on posts but curves upwards and ends on a (near) horizontal line (Fig.3.17). The

66

'gap' between the two ends of the boat is then filled by a full-length strake. A similar planking pattern to that of the Indian reverse-clinker boats is seen on a range of medieval European depictions of a vessel tentatively identified as a *hulc* (see Vol.1, p.160–162), a ship-type often mentioned in medieval accounts.

*3.17. A reverse-clinker nauka under repair near the River Piyain at Bolla Ghat, Sylhet District, Bangladesh.*

## Frame-first vessels

The planked boats discussed earlier in this chapter were built plank-first: that is, the planking was first fashioned and fastened together, thereby determining the shape of the vessel's hull. The alternative sequence is known as 'frame-first': the framework is 'designed' and set up to give the hull shape. Worldwide, the earliest-known vessel built in this sequence appears to be *Blackfriars 1* a seagoing, Romano-Celtic vessel of the mid second century AD, excavated from the River Thames in London.

*3.18. A Tuticorin thoni under all plain sail in Colombo harbour, Sri Lanka in 1994. (Captain A.W. Kinghorn)*

In India, the frame-first sequence has recently begun to be used when building large ships as one element in a process that has included the mechanisation of shipyards and the use of materials other than wood. There are, however, other ships and boats that, in contrast to all other types of traditional vessel on India's Bay of Bengal coast, have, for a considerable time, been built frame-first. These are: two ship types – the Tuticorin *thoni* (Fig.3.18) and the Cuddalore *kotia*; and three boat types- the *vattai* fishing boats of Palk Bay (Fig.3.19), the *vallam* from further south, and the *vattal* dumb lighter of Cuddalore. These Tamil vessels are designed by methods that are very similar to, but a simplification of, those used by early sixteenth-century Portuguese shipbuilders to derive all a hull's frame shapes from the shape of a master frame.

Tuticorin *thoni* are sailing cargo ships of 250 to 650 tonnes capacity with three masts on which can be set twelve, and more, sails: they are used in the Tamil Nadu/Sri Lanka trade. Their framing is designed on a lofting floor using a single, two-part mould and a simple geometric construction that is comparable with, and evidently related to, Venetian/Atlantic methods used in post-medieval Portugal.

The Atirampattinam *vattai* is a fishing boat, some 12 m in length, used in the northern parts of Palk Bay (Fig.3.19). It is double-ended with a high-rising bow, and has a simple hull form with a long, box-like, central part: only in the regions approaching bow and stern, where the hull rises and narrows, does the transverse section change. Thus the builder has to determine the shape of only four frames to fix the entire hull shape. The shape of all fifteen central section frames (known as 'equal' frames) is taken directly from the master mould.

*3.19. A vattai, under foresail and mainsail, taking the ground at the landing place at Eripurakarai, Tamil Nadu.*

*3.20. A scrieve board and a master mould used, in conjunction with a formula, to determine the shape of one half of a pair of vattai un-equal frames: in a boat shed at Atirampattinam, Tamil Nadu.*

The other three frame shapes are derived from that mould using a scrieve board (Fig.3.20) and a 'rule of thumb' which allows for the rising and narrowing of the hull towards the ends of the boat: these three pairs of frames are known as 'unequal' frames. These curves are then transferred to timbers, and fifteen equal frames and three pairs of unequal frames are fashioned.

In both the Tamil design system and in that used in the medieval Mediterranean/Atlantic, the position of the foremost and the aftermost designed frame is emphasised by giving those frames a specific name. Furthermore, there is a remarkable similarity in the way that dove-tail joints are used to join futtocks to floors in the *thoni* and the *vattai*, on the one hand, and in the several sixteenth century wrecks of Iberian ships excavated from American and European waters, on the other. The Tamil design system is a simplification of the Atlantic method, producing less- complex hull forms that are more suitable for the *thoni* and, especially, the *vattai*.

Tamil ships and boats are not fully designed: there is still an element of building 'by eye' and the use of personal experience – for example, when fairing the framework before it is planked, and when determining the run of the sheerline. The Tamil builder also uses his 'art and craft' when he works bevels on the 'unequal' frames, and when he spiles the shapes of the pairs of passive frames from planking used as ribbands.

## PROPULSION AND STEERING

The earliest Indian evidence for propulsion by sail is the mast on the vessel depicted on a pot shard from Mohenjo-Daro dated *c.* 2000 BC (Fig.3.3). The impression gained from a range of later depictions is that such masts were invariably stepped amidships: this means that, in all probability, the single square sail was used. By BC/AD times, there is a sequence of depictions: first with a single square sail; then two masts; and, by the fourth century AD, three masts. The type of sail set by those two- and three-masted ships is not clear. A vessel on one of the Ajanta vases appears to have a lugsail, but this may have been a ship from South-East Asia. Both types of lateen were used in the eastern Mediterranean from late-Roman times onwards, and it is sometimes claimed that the Arab lateen (a *setee* with a short luff) was *the* sail of the Indian Ocean, but this dominance probably did not occur until late-Medieval times. A *patella* drawn by Bowrey in the mid seventeenth century, has a mast stepped well forward which suggests a fore-and-aft sail. In the early nineteenth century, Admiral Pâris recorded a range of sails and rigs on traditional Indian Ocean craft, including spritsails on small boats, square sails on river craft and, at sea, lugsails and both types of lateen.

Two steering oars, one on each quarter, seem to have been the main means of steering Indian seagoing vessels until post-medieval times. Nowadays they are still used on traditional craft: when only one such oar is shipped, it is generally to port.

## THE 'PERIPLUS MARIS ERYTHRAEI'

This Greek text, probably written in *c.* AD 50, is an example of a group of early Mediterranean documents known as *Periploi* ('circum-navigations'). These were written versions of pilotage information that, in earlier times, had been memorized by rote; they were a combination of what would nowadays be called 'a sailing pilot', 'a regional handbook and a 'trading guide'. Descriptions of the harbours along a particular route and pilotage information (directions and distances, landmarks, shoals and other hazards) for that route were included, as were lists of the goods that could be embarked from, or traded with, those harbours.

The '*Periplus Maris Erythrae*i' does not deal merely with the Red Sea as known today, it is also concerned with the western Indian Ocean from Burma to Zanzibar, including the Persian Gulf. Its unknown author came from Egypt and was probably a trader who may himself have sailed to India as far south, perhaps, as the 'pepper coast' of Travancore.

Two coastal routes from harbours on Egypt's Red Sea coast are described (Fig.1.10 or 2.9): the first takes the vessel from *Myos Hormos* along the western coast of the Red Sea and the coast of Sudan/Eritrea; then round the Horn of Africa (Somalia) and south to the Zanzibar region; the second route, beginning at Berenicê, also takes the ship southwards through the Red Sea; then eastwards along the southern coast of Arabia (leaving the Persian Gulf to port); and continues coastwise to India and beyond. As an alternative to this coastal passage, an open-sea passage to the Indian west coast, using the south-west monsoon, is given. In earlier days, *Eudaimon Arabia* (Aden) was the point of departure for such a passage. At the time that this *periplus* was compiled, however, two places further east were used: Kanê (probably *Hisne Ghurab*) *c.* 200 nm east of Aden; and *Aramaton Emporion*, near Cape Guardafui the north-west tip of the Horn of Africa.

The author of this *periplus* believed that 'Hippalus' was the name of the first Greek seaman to use such an open-sea route to India (in fact, his name was probably 'Eudoxus'). Pliny (*NH* 6.26.100), on the other hand, considered '*Hippalus*' was the Arabic term for the south-west monsoon, a conjecture that proved correct. Moreover, Pliny (*NH* 6.26.99-105) described different sea passages from those in the *Periplus*: early voyagers to India took departure from *Suagros* (Ras Fartak, a prominent cape on the Arabian Hadramaut coast) and sailed with the monsoon wind to *Patale* near the Indus delta – this destination was later changed to *Sigerus* (Jaigarh, 120 nm south of Bombay). Subsequently the route started from *Ocelis* (Sheikh Sa'id, at the mouth of the Red Sea in the Bab el Mandeb) to *Muziris* (Cranganore on India's western coast); then further south to *Becarê* (Pirakad) on the Malabar coast. It seems clear that, as new opportunities in southern India became known to Mediterranean merchants, navigators altered their point of departure to optimise direct passages to Indian harbours further south.

## SEAFARING
### The Arabian Sea
The *Periplus* (Ch. 24, 39, 49 and 56) tells us that ships planning to cross the Arabian Sea to India should leave Egypt in July. They would thus sail through the Gulf of Aden and the Arabian Sea in August and September when they would have a fair monsoon wind and less boisterous seas. It would also have been prudent to arrive in southern Indian waters in late-September since, as Pliny (*NH* 6.24.83) relates, the west coasts of India and Sri Lanka had especially stormy seas during the three months between mid-June and mid-September when ships arriving there would have faced a lee shore with strong winds. Off-shore sailing did not usually become practicable until the end of August in the northern sector, the end of September off Bombay, and the end of October on the Malabar Coast.

The *Periplus* does not state how long such open sea passages took, but Pliny (*NH* 6. 26) states that sailing with the south-west monsoon from *Ocelis* (Cella ), it took forty days to reach *Muziris* (Cranganore on the Malabar coast). The two knots average speed that this indicates is probably due to having to make ground to the south, away from Arabia, before turning north-east and running with the monsoon.

The timing of return voyages is not mentioned in the *Periplus*, however, Pliny states that ships left India with the south-east wind in

December or early January. The Arabian Sea is dominated by the north-east monsoon from late-November until March, and ships heading for the Gulf of Aden would have had the wind on their starboard beam. Not until January or February, when approaching north-east Africa or the southern Arabian coast, would they have had a favourable south-east wind. This would have been followed, in the Red Sea, by a fair southerly wind. Overall, a voyage from Egypt to India and return could therefore have been accomplished in about eight months, from July to March.

The Bay of Bengal

The largest vessels working these waters are said to have been *kolandiophonta*: a term that may have been derived from the Chinese *kun lun po* applied to non-Chinese ships trading in South-East Asia. Sangara, local craft of the Coromandel coast, are mentioned in Ch. 60 of the *Erythrean Periplus*: this term is related to Tamil *Shangadam*: a log raft. The term *sangara/shangadam* was borrowed by sixteenth century Portuguese as *jangada* and applied to the seagoing log rafts of Brazil. Today, log rafts in the Laccadive Islands are known as *sangadam*.

The earliest (second century AD?) overseas trading between India and South-East Asia appears to have been undertaken on coastal passages from Orissa via Bengal to lower Burma. Similarities between artifacts excavated on the west coast of northern Java and those from Tamil coastal sites suggest that this coastal route was subsequently extended along the west coast of Malaya to the Indonesian islands, and subsequently to the Mekong valley in Viet Nam: two coins from excavations in Thailand have depictions of a ship said to be similar to those on Palava coins from the Coromandel coast. In later years, the Indian sector of this coastal route was extended southwards from Orissa to landing places in the rivers Krishna and Godavari in Andrha Pradesh, and on into Tamil Nadu.

It may be that direct passages across the Bay of Bengal – eastwards and south-eastwards, from southern India and Sri Lanka to the Malay peninsula and Sumatra (or from east to west?) – were attempted at an early date, but this would seem unlikely before vessels were built capable not only of withstanding the rigours of a five or six weeks ocean passage, but also able to sail closer to the wind than on a broad reach. A direct, open sea, passage – but in a different direction – may have been undertaken during the fifth/sixth centuries AD when Madagascar, off the eastern African coast, was colonised from South-East Asia (possibly from southern Borneo). On such an ocean passage, the south-east trades or the north-east monsoon would have facilitated a near-equatorial, westward-bound route between Sumatra and Sri Lanka. The alternative was the well-established coastal route, anticlockwise around the Bay of Bengal to Sri Lanka.

In the ninth and tenth centuries AD, Arab navigational abilities expanded dramatically (see p.40–43) and, by the tenth century, Arab seamen were regularly sailing to all parts of the Indian Ocean. It may be that some of those passages were direct from Sri Lanka to Sumatra, rather than coastwise. The difficulties encountered on such an open sea voyage were experienced by Tim Severin during his sewn-plank boat passage from Sri Lanka to the western entrance to the Malacca Strait, north of Sumatra.

## PILOTAGE AND NAVIGATION
Suparagā, of the first century AD compiled a Sanscript text in which he described the capabilities of an Arabian Sea pilot: "— he knows the course of the stars and can always orientate himself; he knows the value of signs, both regular, accidental and abnormal, of good and bad weather; he distinguishes the regions of the oceans by the fish, the colour of the water, the nature of the bottom, the birds, the mountains and other indications." Furthermore, Pliny (*NH* 6.24.83) reported that Sri Lankan seaman used shore-sighting birds to find the direction of land. Similar practices had been noted in the fifth century BC *Kevaddha Sutta* of Digha and in the Hindu *Sutta Pitaka*. Such non-instrumental navigational techniques were used worldwide until medieval times and, indeed, into the twentieth century in parts of India. *Periploi* included useful pilotage information: for example, the *Periplus Maris Erythraei* stated that approach to the River Indus could be recognised when still out of sight of land by a distinctively coloured

outflow of water; moreover, sea snakes could be seen. Pilots were also advised that *Barbariké* (a harbour in the Indus delta) was near a small island up the middle channel of the seven channels forming the delta of the River Sinthus (Indus).

Pliny (*NH* 6.21) noted that the overall length of the west coast of India (2,850 n.m.) was '40 days' sail': thus his standard "day's sail" was *c.* 72 nm. Distances between ports are sometimes given: for example, it is said to be 3,000 *stades* (*c.* 300 nautical miles) from Barbariké to Astakapra (Hathab), a harbour opposite Barugaza (Broach) in the Gulf of Cambay, The actual distance from Barbariké to Broach is *c.* 400 nm but it is *c.* 300 nm from Barbariké to the entrance to the Gulf of Cambay.

*Barugaza* is described in some detail in the *Periplus* (chs. 41-46), indicating that, in those days, it was an important east coast harbour. It is said to be about 300 *stades* (30 nm) up the River *Lamnaios* (Narbada); the mouth of that river is difficult to find since the coast thereabouts is low lying and there are shoals in the vicinity. The approach to *Barugaza* is also said to be difficult because of the narrowness of the bay and strong currents. Moreover, there is a great tidal range there, with correspondingly strong tidal streams: boats may be capsized and ships may be driven onto shoals and wrecked. These effects are especially serious at the time of new moon when a tidal bore (or *egre*) can be both heard and seen rushing in from seaward with the flood tide. Because of such problems *Arlake,* ruler of that region, sends pilots in oared boats to guide visiting ships into the river on the flood tide so that they moor at *Barugaza* around the time of high water. When necessary, pilot boats tow visiting ships to their berth.

Pliny's (*NH* 6.24.82) remark that the distance from Ceylon to the River Ganges was equivalent to seven days' sail 'by our ships', shows that, by the first century AD, Roman ships had rounded Cape Comorin and sailed into the Bay of Bengal (Strabo:15. 686). By AD 166 they had sailed beyond Burma to Malaysia, and possibly as far as Indo-China.

The pilotage and non-instrumental methods of navigation used in Indian waters during the Graeco-Roman period continued in use through medieval times and (by fishermen) into the twentieth century.

Navigational treatise by medieval Arab seamen and astronomers are known, from the time when instruments began to be used, but there are no Indian equivalents. It is therefore not possible to estimate how much Indian seamen contributed to the development of instrumental navigation. It seems clear, however, that Indian methods were similar to those used by Arabs. For example, Indians and Arabs used the *zam* unit of distance and the *isba* unit of angular measurement. In fact, Dr. Aleem has suggested that the *zam* was an Indian unit adopted by Arabs. Mid seventeenth century sailing manuals, formerly used by Gujarat seamen, have survived: these include summaries of astronomical observations, coastal profiles showing features near landing places, and diagrammatic charts with annotated routes marked on them. By this date, at the latest, Indian seamen were clearly in step with their contemporaries in their use of pilotage and navigational techniques.

Harbours

The *Periplus* (Chs 52, 53) mentions thirteen landing places south of the Gulf of Cambay including *Kalliena* (Kalyana), in what is now Bombay harbour. Further south was *Mouziris* (Cranganore on the River Periyar) one of the destinations of ships from Egypt (Pliny *NH* 6.26). *Komar* (*Periplus* ch. 58), a harbour with a fort and an important religious settlement, is believed to have been at or near Cape Comorin (Pliny's *Coliacum*), the southernmost point of India. This would have been a difficult cape to round, but this aspect is not mentioned in the *Periplus*. This omission and the fact that nothing is said about sewn plank boats (known to have been extensively used, from the sixteenth century, on the south Kerala and the Coromandel coasts) may indicate that the author had no personal knowledge of India beyond Bakaré (Vaikkarai – between Quilon and Trivandrum).

The island of *Palaisimoundou* formerly *Taprobanê* (Sri Lanka) is mentioned in Ch. 61, and *Poduké* (probably Arikamedu near Pondicherry) and *Sopatma* (near Madras) on the Coromandel coast of Tamil Nadu in Ch. 60. *Masilia* (Masulipatnam) is mentioned in Ch. 62 and, in Ch. 63, a port in the Ganges delta is noted but not named: it is said to have an annual flooding season like the Nile.

# CHAPTER 4

# Australia

Thereere were seamen before there were farmers, boat-builders before there were wainwrights, and there were early navigators who could keep their reckoning across the trackless sea without charts or any of the other navigational aids we have today. Amongst the earliest seafarers were the people who first populated Australia, sometime between 60,000 and 40,000 BC, when sea level was much lower than today (Fig.4.1). In those times, Borneo, Sumatra, Java and nearby places that are now islands were all part of mainland South-East Asia; moreover, New Guinea and adjacent islands were connected to Australia. Between that south-eastern extension to Asia ("Sundaland") and Greater Australia ("Sahulland") lay an archipelago of islands ('Wallacia'), 600 nautical miles (1,100 km) in length, so disposed that from a boat in the coastal waters of an island off Borneo further islands to the south-east could be seen. Such inter-island visibility persisted across this archipelago so that, at each stage of migration, land was in sight, ahead or astern.

That migration from Asia to Australia probably took place over a period of many generations and, although no water transport of that age has been excavated, the series of passages through Indonesian waters ("Wallacia") has been partly documented by early sites along this route with evidence for human occupation.

## THE EARLIEST SEA PASSAGES
Using Bio-geographic data, this region (South-East Asia to Australia) is conveniently divided into three areas (Fig.4.1).

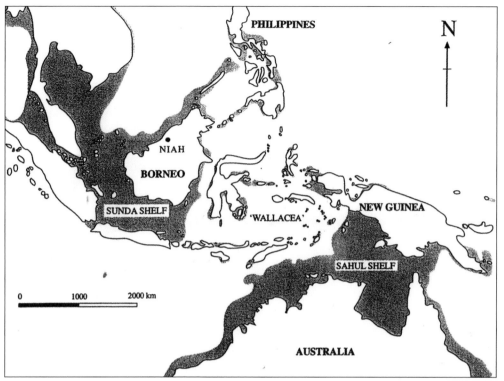

*4.1. Map showing the deduced coastlines of South-east Asia and Australia in c. 30,000 BC, a time of very low sea-levels. The Wallacean archipelago lies between the Sunda shelf and the Sahul shelf. The shaded areas are now under the sea.*

### 'Sundaland'

At times of lower sea levels, 'Sundaland' extended as a continuation of the present-day mainland South-East Asia to a transition zone (the 'Huxley' line) running from the Pacific westwards between Taiwan and the Philippines; southward across the Sulu sea; between Borneo and Sulawesi; between Bali and Lombok; and on into the Indian Ocean.

### 'Sahulland'

Also known as 'Greater Australia'. At times of lower sea level this region extended from the Tropics in New Guinea and northern

Australia to temperate Tasmania in the south. Thus, New Guinea, Australia, Tasmania and many smaller islands formed one land-mass that extended as far westward as the 'Weber' line running from the Indian Ocean east of Timor, north-eastwards through the Banda Sea; west of New Guinea and east of the Moluccas, and on into the Pacific.

'Wallacea'
This is the name given to the archipelago of islands between Sundaland and Sahulland (i.e. between the Huxley and the Weber lines). Geological and biogeographical evidence shows that, even at times of lowest sea level, this has always been an archipelago, thus migration from Sundaland to Sahulland must have involved several sea passages through that group of islands.

Islands visible from Sundaland, or of which there was 'early warning', would probably have been visited several times before the decision was made to settle there. Subsequently, similar exploratory voyages would have been undertaken to islands further east – and so on until Greater Australia was reached. There would have been no dramatic environmental changes to cope with since the coastal lands of north-west Greater Australia had a similar range of marine life to that in the Indonesian islands, although some adaptation would have been needed when the south of Australia was reached.

**MIGRATION ROUTES** (Fig.4.2)
Although the precise date and route of this migration are not certain, there is general agreement that the migrants originally came from Taiwan or the south-east coast of China. Two possible routes across the Wallacean archipelago have been identified: a northern route from Borneo to New Guinea via Sulawesi and the Moluccas, and a southern route from Java through Flores and Timor to north-west Australia.

At times of lowest sea level (circa 53,000 and 18,000 BC), the longest individual passage would have been *c.* 60 nautical miles (100 km): using paddles, such a crossing would have taken about two days. Human survival would have mainly depended on the carriage of sufficient fresh water; structural survival would have been determined

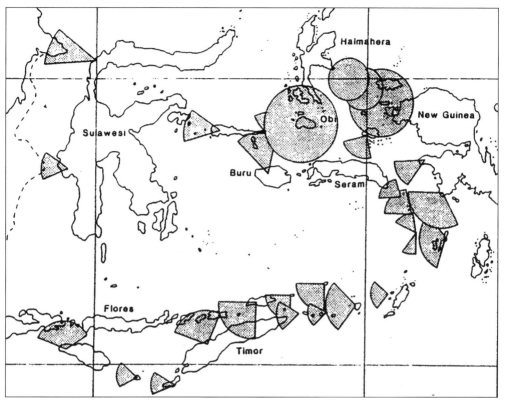

*4.2. Map showing visibility sectors along northern and southern routes across the Wallacean archipelago. (After Irwin)*

by the boat-building materials used and on the weather experienced – the best season would have been a period of calm, settled weather with good visibility.

## NAVIGATION

In those early days, pilotage methods (land always in sight) would have been used. Some authors have argued that exploratory voyages would not have been made unless there was 'two-way visibility' between islands: that is, 'Newland' to the east could be seen from sea level when still ashore in 'Homeland' – in other words, throughout every passage, both 'Homeland' and 'Newland' could be seen. A less restrictive approach is to assume that such voyages were undertaken when there was 'one-way' visibility: although 'Newland' could not be seen from sea level while ashore in 'Homeland', it could be seen by explorers afloat before they lost sight of 'Homeland'. Moreover, the existence of 'Newland' could have already been established, either visually from a high point in 'Homeland', or by the indirect methods described in Chapter 1 of the companion volume to this book that deals with Europe.

With either type of visibility, visual pilotage methods would have been used to 'plot' the vessel's position. Some of these crossings included night travel: on a clear, tropical night, it would probably have been possible to maintain visual contact with either 'Homeland' or 'Newland'. Nevertheless, the possibility of poor visibility, by night or by day, may well have led to the development of ways of maintaining a heading by reference to the swell, the wind or even the stars.

**WATER TRANSPORT**
Remains of the water transport used by these pioneering seamen have not been excavated, Aboriginal oral histories do not illuminate the matter, and depictions of craft are no earlier than the eighteenth century A.D. The earliest, reliable evidence for early Australian water transport comes in descriptions compiled by Europeans in the seventeenth and eighteenth centuries, at the time of 'first contact'. Tasmania is especially important in this context since it became isolated from mainland Australia by rising sea levels before 7,000 BC i.e. at about the time that New Guinea separated from Australia.

Tasmanian floats and rafts
The Tasmanian tool kit consisted of scrapers and simple percussion and bone tools; they never had hafted tools which appeared in mainland Australia around 3,000 BC and enabled mainlanders to build advanced forms of log raft and bark boat. With their elementary tool kit, Tasmanians built log floats, log rafts, and seagoing bundle rafts.

*Log floats*

Single driftwood logs were used to cross rivers. Similar logs were used to visit islands off the north-west coast of Australia: withies were twined around wooden pegs driven into both sides of such logs to form stabilisers at the waterline and also to be used as a foot rest.

*Log rafts*

Although doubts have been expressed about the accuracy of early-nineteenth century accounts of log rafts off the Tasmanian coasts, it is now generally agreed that two-log rafts (the simplest possible) were indeed made. The logs were linked together by several transverse timbers which were lashed in position by bark strips. As Tasmanians appear to have had no tools that could fell trees, it seems likely that they used fire, or 'harvested' driftwood or logs that had been blown down by the wind.

*Bundle rafts*

Tasmanians occasionally made rafts from reeds using five bundles of bulrushes (*Typha* sp.). However, they principally made them from bark bundles (Fig, 4.3), a use not known elsewhere in the world. The bark so used was either 'stringy-bark' *Eucalyptus oblique* or *regnans* or 'paper bark' (*Melaleuca* sp.). A paper bark raft weighed 350 lbs (160 kg) compared with the 500 lbs (230 kg) of a stringy-bark raft of similar size. Moreover, the paper bark was more resistant to waterlogging. Loose pieces of bark, picked up from the ground or pulled from the tree trunk, were used so a specialised de-barking tool (used in Australia and in North America) was not needed in Tasmania. Individual pieces of bark were bundled together and bound by a rope of grass or inner bark into bundles that tapered towards each end. Three bundles were lashed together with the two smaller bundles outboard of, and above, the larger bundle, thereby forming a boat-shaped raft with upturned ends. Early-nineteenth century bark rafts were *c.* 10 ft long by 3–4 ft broad, with an inside depth of 10 in (3 x 0.9–1.2 x 0.025 m); the largest known was 15 x 5 ft (4.5 x 1.5 m). In the shallows these rafts were steered and propelled by poles; in deeper water, poles were plied like

*4.3. Early-19<sup>th</sup> century Tasmanian bark bundle rafts.*

double-bladed paddles. Alternatively, rafts were hand paddled, or pulled and pushed by swimmers. Progress against the wind was always difficult.

Rafts were soon waterlogged: it has been estimated that a paper bark raft would have insufficient buoyancy after five or six hours, whereas a stringy-bark raft would reach this state in less than an hour. Rafts were mainly used to cross bays and rivers. If those waterlogging estimates are correct, voyages of five miles or so, out to an island, would have had to be undertaken on a paper bark raft, rather than a stringy-bark raft, and with a fair wind and a favourable current.

### Australian rafts
In Australia, on the other hand, three types of log raft have been documented: river rafts and single and double rafts for inshore waters.

*River rafts*

Simple, often ephemeral, river rafts were used in eastern Queensland and along the north coast. Several mangrove saplings were lashed together at the ends, using bark strips or grass cord. Logs were positioned relative to one another so that a 'boat- shape' was achieved: the bow became narrower and the raft assumed a slightly-hollowed form.

*Seagoing rafts*

The simplest version of these rafts was 6–7 ft (1.8–2.1 m) long, made of mangrove logs fastened together by hardwood treenails about 1ft (0.30 m) in length. The butt end of each log was placed at one end to make a trapezoidal shape with a narrow bow. Towards the other end, pegs were driven into the logs to form a circular enclosure in which fishing tackle and fish could be stowed – a wooden 'tub' was similarly used in recent Taiwanese log rafts. A more complex version was made of two rafts. A seven-log, single raft was positioned so that its narrower end partly overlapped the narrow end of a nine-log raft. The rafts were not fastened together, but kept in contact by the weight of the upper raft and the one or two-man crew. Such composite rafts were used for fishing, hunting turtles and exploring islands up to ten nautical miles (16 km) offshore. A paddle, made from the lower stem of a mangrove and with the fan-shaped root forming the blade, was used both to steer and to propel this double raft into, and out of, tidal flows which were their main means of propulsion. A turtle spear, thrust down between the logs, was used to moor them.

Australian bark boats

Bark boats were used on the rivers, and in the coastal waters, of Victoria, New South Wales, Queensland and the Northern Territory. The bark came from the stringy-bark tree (*Eucalyptus oblique*) or the river red gum (*Eucalyptus camaldulensis*). During the rainy season, in late Spring/early Summer, when the sap was flowing, bark was prised from bole using  special wedges and levers. Sometimes a complete cylinder was cut, thereby killing the tree, but most were made from half- cylinder strips. Eight to ten men could be needed to lower the larger strips to the ground. Three types of bark boat were built: simple; lashed; and stitched.

*Simple bark boats*
In the Murray/Darling basin, in western Victoria, a thickish slab of bark, shaped like an open-ended trough, was fitted with a few transverse sticks to prevent the bark curling further and used as a boat in still waters. If required for more-demanding tasks, the ends were blocked with clay or mud. Such a boat could be assembled in less than half a day.

*Lashed bark boats* (Fig.4.4)
The lashed boats, of the rivers and creeks of New South Wales and south-west Victoria, were of a different standard. The outer surface of the bark was removed and the ends thinned to produce a thin sheet

*4.4. Early-19$^{th}$ century Australian lashed bark boats.*

which was then heated to make it pliable. The bark sheet was then turned inside out and moulded in the ground to a deeper shape with upturned ends which were then pleated, bunched and tied with bark cord. A few rod stretchers and some cord ties were next fitted to maintain the hull shape and to keep the sides a fixed distance apart. Superior models, carrying at least two men, had occasional, flexible ribs, and a sapling or a cylindrical bundle of rushes was added along the top of each side to stiffen the rim.

*Stitched bark boats*
Sewn bark boats were the most advanced of Australian craft, comparable in their general structure with American bark boats. They were built from several bark sheets sewn together with bark strips or bast cord. A typical one would be made from seven segments of eucalyptus bark: one long, wide sheet for one side of the boat, two wide pieces for the other; and two pointed pieces at each end where they were made up-rising. After being moulded to shape, these bark pieces were stitched together, and the seams were caulked with gum. A supporting framework of stretchers, ties and ribs was then inserted within the bark hull. The largest boats known measured 16–18 ft. x *c.*2 ft (4.88–5.49 x 0.60 m); they carried a crew of eight.

Logboats
Outrigger craft – probably logboats with washstrakes – were seen off Cape York Peninsula by Captain Cook on his first voyage in 1770. These are thought to have come from New Guinea and Makassar in Sulawesi. Malay seaman occasionally visited Australia during the fifteenth to the seventeenth centuries AD, and introduced logboat building, and possibly the sail, to the Northern Territory. These techniques appear not to have spread outside a few isolated places on Australia's northern coast.

**EARLY SEAFARING**
The floats, rafts and boats observed during the period of early European contact matched the way of life then being pursued by

indigenous Australians and Tasmanians. None of these craft, however, appear to match the specification for the type of seagoing vessel needed to cross the Wallacean archipelago. It is questionable whether any of them would have maintained their structural integrity for the one or two days needed to undertake passages between islands. An alternative explanation could be that, after the lengthy migration from Sundaland to Sahulland had been completed and the stimulus of a requirement for lengthy, sea voyages had disappeared, the art of building substantial water transport was foregone. The standard of raft and boat-building may have regressed until it matched a new maximum requirement: voyages of up to 20 nautical miles (32 km) – a performance that was attained by Australia's (but not Tasmania's) technologically-advanced, bark boats in the Gulf of Carpentaria, as noted in first contact accounts.

None of the indigenous types of water transport recently used in Australia and Tasmania were suitable for crossing the Wallacean archipelago. Australian water transport noted at first contact was built from logs, reed bundles or bark – these raw materials were also available in prehistoric Sundaland. As Wallacea lies within the Tropics, rafts could have been used at sea. For long-range sea passages, reeds in bundle rafts have to resist waterlogging: this can be achieved by choosing a particular harvesting season; binding the bundles tightly to achieve maximum compression and rigidity; and forming them into a 'boat-shaped' raft. To maximise seagoing performance, log rafts similarly should be boat-shaped and the chosen log species has to be relatively lightweight and resistant to waterlogging. Such techniques would have been compatible with the Palaeolithic technology of the early migrants from Sundaland.

The most technologically-advanced boat built in Australia (not in Tasmania) was a particular type of bark boat. Worldwide, bark boats are generally not used at sea, even in recent memory: the most-advanced, North American bark boat was not truly seagoing, though it is known to have undertaken passages in an estuary-type of environment within the Gulf of St Lawrence between Newfoundland and Labrador. Moreover, it seems unlikely that such boats could be built using Palaeolithic techniques. Bundle rafts are known to have been used in Oceania, but they have not been noted in Sundaland, although reed is readily available there. Bark-built, and bundle-built vessels are therefore unlikely to have been used to cross Wallacea. Logboats are also doubtful: they were not found in indigenous use at first contact in Australia: and the woodworking techniques needed to build a seagoing logboat are unlikely to have been available in Palaeolithic times. Seagoing rafts made of logs, on the other hand, require rope-making, lashing and binding techniques, rather than advanced woodworking. They are, and have been, widely used in coastal Asia, from western India to China, and also in Oceania.

The seagoing rafts of northern Vietnam and Taiwan are made of twelve or more, large bamboos lashed together in a boat shape. On balances, similar rafts seem most likely to have been used by migrants crossing the Wallacean archipelago. Bamboo is not indigenous to Australia, but it grows, and probably formerly grew, in China, Vietnam, Java and generally along the proposed northern migration route to Sahulland. It is strong yet lightweight, its silica-coated exterior delays waterlogging, and it can readily be lashed together.

The second requirement for the trans-Wallacean migration was to be able to hold a heading at night. Although at first contact, Australian and Tasmanian rafts and boats were never observed more than about twenty miles from land, Aborigine landsmen undoubtedly had the ability to find their way about Australia's desert interior, an achievement similar in some respects to holding a course at sea. It is not unreasonable, therefore, to suggest that, in earlier times, after dark, they could have steered a course relative to wind, swell or the stars. The Wallacean archipelago could have been crossed using visual navigation, but when necessary, these pioneering explorers would have used simple environmental navigation methods to keep their reckoning and hold their course.

# CHAPTER 5

# South-East Asia

T his chapter deals with the Malay peninsula, the Gulf of Thailand, the myriad islands of the Indo-Malaysian archipelago (including the Philippines) and the lower reaches and deltas of three great rivers: Chao Phraya, in Thailand; Mekong in Cambodia; and the River Red that flows into the Gulf of Tongking (Fig.5.1). The region stretches from 95° to 135° E, and from 20° N, across the equator, to 12ºS and many of the islands within the main archipelago are intervisible: in early times this may well have been a 'nursery' for boatbuilding and seafaring innovations.

That part of the region within 5° of the Equator has an equatorial climate with several predominant winds: away from this zone there is a tropical climate with clearly defined wet and dry seasons. NNE monsoon winds prevail from October to April, when it is dry and cool; during May to September, the northern summer months, it is hot and wet and SSW winds predominate.

Hardwoods and bamboos suitable for building rafts and boats are widely available throughout the region. From *c.* 8,000 BC, mats, ropes and baskets were made from rattan palms and *pandanus* leaves. In recent times, sails have been made from matting, and boats have been built using basketry techniques Moreover, resins and dammar from tropical trees are readily available to make boats watertight; such practices may well have prehistoric origins.

Between 18,000 BC and 3,000 BC rising sea levels reduced the land area but increased, by a multiple of three, the ratio of length of coastline to area of land. Towards the end of that period seasonal flooding, originating in the Himalayas, established substantial deltas in the lower reaches of the three major rivers and, by 3000 BC, with

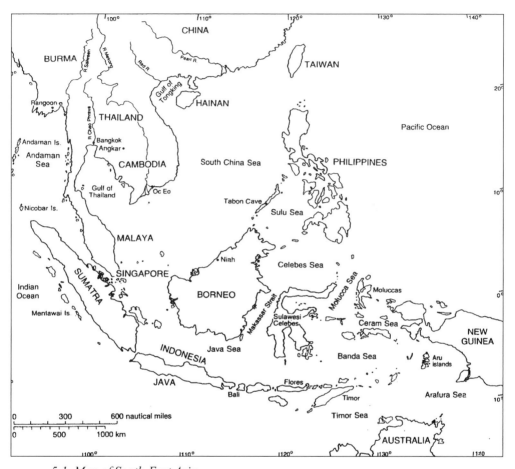

*5.1. Map of South-East Asia.*

mean sea level within today's tidal range, the coastlines of maritime South-East Asia appeared much as they do today.

## AUSTRONESIAN MIGRATIONS

Archaeological data and other information indicate that, between 4500 and 4000 BC, Austronesian-speaking, Neolithic peoples migrated from south China to Taiwan. By *c.* 3000BC they had expanded to Luzon, in the northern Philippines, and, by 2500 BC, had settled the Philippines and the islands of Borneo and Sulawasi; from there, they moved to the rest of maritime, South-East Asia. Subsequently, in the mid-second Millennium BC, Austronesians began to colonise Oceania (see p.129–133) and then, in the early centuries AD, Madagascar off the east African coast. These migrations must have been undertaken by water transport, but the earliest-known boat remains in South-East Asia are no earlier than the early centuries AD. The boat type that has become characteristic of this region – the plank boat fitted with double outriggers – is unlikely to have been the boat of the earliest migrations since there is no evidence there, or anywhere in the world, for plank-built boats before the Bronze Age. Moreover, there is no evidence for the use of outriggers in South-East Asia until the late first Millennium AD. The craft most likely to have been used by the earliest seafarers in South-East Asia appears to be the log raft or possibly boats of basketry or of bark.

**EARLY MARITIME CONTACTS**

The Graeco-Roman world imported raw materials and manufactured goods from South-East Asia, although, in the early days of this trade, it was probably through Indian emporia. By the second century AD, however, Roman vessels had reached Malaya, and possibly Indo-China. Vessels in this overseas trade were naturally funnelled through the Malacca strait, between western Malaya and eastern Sumatra where there were informal landing places. The trading town of *Oc Eo*, in Vietnam's Mekong delta was one of the earliest urban settlements in SE Asia: it may well have been the *Funan*, mentioned in Chinese accounts.

Locked mortise and tenon joints (a sign of Mediterranean boatbuilding practices) had been used to fasten together the planking of a number of boats, dating from the first century BC to second century AD, that have been excavated in Vietnam and Malaya. Moreover, a thirteenth century Philippines wreck, *Butuan 2*, had locked-treenail plank fastenings, possibly an adaptation of Roman technology.

Overseas trade between South-East Asia and China appears to have been established by the third century BC. South-East Asian ships regularly visited southern Chinese ports, mainly to embark Buddhist pilgrims for Sumatra and India. Chinese interest in trade with South-East Asia increased during the Song Dynasties (tenth to thirteenth centuries), the Chinese being particularly interested in produce from the Moluccas (the 'spice islands').

## WATER TRANSPORT

A number of representations of boats, of various dates, are known from this region, but most of these stone carvings, rock paintings and metal engravings cannot be unambiguously interpreted. Moreover, unlike their neighbours in China, South-East Asia has no early tradition of literacy so that there are no indigenous descriptions of water transport or seafaring, although something may be learned from Chinese and, to a lesser extent, from Indian, sources and also from the observations of informed travellers in the early-nineteenth century. Moreover, during the past 150 years, several seagoing ships have been excavated in this region. Indonesia now has the largest fleet of working, sailing vessels in the world: an array of traditional rafts and boats displaying fittings and features of rig and of construction that may well have survived from earlier days.

Log rafts.

No log rafts have been excavated but, among the stone reliefs in the eighth to ninth century Candi Buddhist temple at Borobodur in Java, there are several depicting what appear to be boat-shaped, log rafts each fitted with an outrigger (possibly two) of several logs (Fig.5.2). These rafts are propelled by canted rectangular sails on two bipod (possibly tripod) masts with a small square-sail on a bowsprit, and are steered by a rudder on each quarter.

During the early nineteenth century, Admiral Pâris noted that log rafts were used for river and harbour fishing in the Philippines. The admiral also published paintings of small boats of Manila and Java that had nine bamboo stabilisers fastened to each side at the waterline which were used as poling walkways and to carry cargo. Effectively,

*5.2. A boat-shaped log raft with an outrigger, depicted under sail on the 8ᵗʰ/9ᵗʰ century Candi, Buddhist temple, Borobudur, Java.*

these craft were log rafts surrounding a central hull. James Hornell, the pioneering, early-twentieth century boat ethnographer, also noted that log rafts were widely used on the lakes and rivers of island South-East Asia, and that linguistic evidence pointed to their earlier use in Java and the Philippines.

A possible descendent of those early rafts is the *ghe be*, a twentieth century bamboo log raft of the coasts and rivers of northern Vietnam. To make such a raft, ten or so, long bamboos are bent under heat and held together by curved transverse bamboos lashed to them, so that the raft is given both transverse and longitudinal curvature. Since the outer, longitudinal bamboos are bigger than the others, these rafts also have slightly-raised 'sides'. Three pole masts, each rigged with a lugsail, are stepped in the transverse bamboos. When not under sail, rafts are propelled by a stern sweep which has a primary, steering role. _Guares_ (wooden fins) are deployed to variable depths, through the bamboo logs, to assist steering and to combat leeway (see p.54, 109–111, 165–166).

## Bark boats

Bark boats are known to have been used in the early twentieth century in Malaya, Borneo and Java: earlier use seems likely. Nishimura, a Japanese observer, noted that the ends of a cylinder of bark were sewn together by Borneo _Dyaks_, and then caulked with clay to form a watertight bow and stern. Light, transverse timbers were subsequently inserted to keep the sides a fixed distance apart.

## Basket boats

Today, Vietnam is the principal area where boats are made of water-proofed basketry (Fig.5.3). No basket boat has been excavated and there are no reports on them dated earlier than the early nineteenth century, nevertheless, the materials, techniques and tool kit needed to build these boats are such that much-earlier use seems likely. Today,

*5.3. A twentieth century, small, Vietnamese basket boat.*

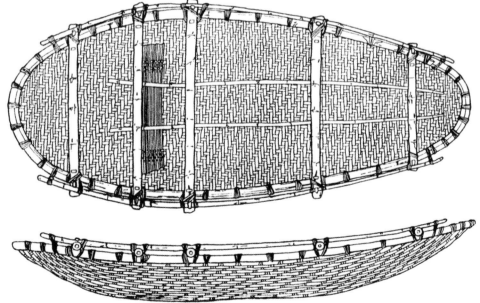

two principal shapes of boat are built: either round in plan (up to 2 m in diameter) or elliptical (the largest being *c.* 4 x 1.25 x 0.65 m). Structurally such boats are the equivalent of hide boats in other regions: a framework (basketry rather than wooden) is made watertight by a paying / caulking of a resin-based mixture (rather than by hide).

Narrow strips of split bamboo are closely woven into a stiff matting to form the basketry hull which is topped by a 'gunwale' of broad bands of split bamboo, bound together with rattan strips. The hull is further supported by bamboo cross-beams fastened by lashings and treenails. On each side, above these beams, a longitudinal bamboo pole is lashed as a 'top rail'. Inboard, along the bottom of the boat either side of her centre line, two further bamboos are fastened as stringers. After the resin-based mixture has been applied inboard and outboard, there is a final coating of vegetable oil. Such a hull is not only watertight but also supple and resilient, able to absorb movement within the basketry without the paying cracking.

In some of the larger basket boats, a light pole rigged with a lugsail of palm-leaf fibres is stepped in a timber on the boat's bottom, and supported higher up by a plank lashed to the 'rim' of the boat. Alternatively, boats are propelled by a paddle over the bow (the narrower end) or by an oar over the stern; in shallow waters, they may be poled. Sailing basket boats have a deep rudder at the stern, and a wooden fin (*guares*) at the bow where it is wedged within a vertical groove: fully down, when close-hauled; part down, on a reach; up, when running free.

These boats are used on Vietnamese rivers, and sometimes a mile or two out to sea, mainly for fishing but also to tend river-grown, rice crops and to harvest water vegetables. Occasionally, two of the elliptical boats are rigged as a pair, linked by a wooden platform fastened across boats about a metre apart. Propelled by sweeps on each quarter, such a composite boat carried horses, their riders and equipment across rivers. Another form of composite boat has treenail-fastened, wooden topsides, above basketry underwater parts. This is larger than the simple basket boat, has a more substantial framing and is used for a wider range of tasks.

Logboats

In the 1950s, excavations in the Niah caves of Sarawak revealed many second to first Millennium BC graves of skeletons in log coffins that formerly had been logboats (Fig.5.4): similar burials were subsequently found in the Philippines, Malaya and Vietnam. In the early nineteenth century, simple logboats, some with added stabilisers at the waterline, were in widespread use on the rivers and sheltered waters of this region. Expanded logboats were also noted in Thailand, on Malayan rivers and in the Mergui archipelago off Malaya's west coast. Several Malayan logboats have been excavated: one of them, from Tanjong Rawa, dated to the second/third century AD, was 5.6 m (18 ft) long but incomplete. This boat had sets of integral, vertically-disposed cleats along its length, sets being 0.60 m (2 ft) apart. Washstrakes could

*5.4. Logboats used as coffins: revealed during excavations in the Niah caves, Sarawak in the 1950s.*

have been fastened to flexible ribs through these cleats, thus increasing the logboat's freeboard. Similar cleats are also a characteristic feature of South-East Asian plank boats: flexible ribs were lashed to them, thereby forcing the boat's planking together.

<u>Planked vessels</u>
*Sewn-planks*
Between 1926 and 1990, several boats with their planking fastened (at least partly) by sewing were excavated in this region: the earliest, from the period AD 260–430, was found within the river bank at Pontian in South Pahang, Malaya. The remains consisted of part of a plank-keel, an end post, three strakes of 50 mm (2 in) thickness, and parts of seven framing timbers. Flush-laid planks were fastened together by a series of individual lashings, two between each side timber: these lashings passed through L-shaped holes within the plank thickness. Treenails, at a wider spacing, protruded through the plank edges: they had been used to position each flush-laid plank before it was fastened in position by the lashings. Framing timbers were lashed to cleats that had been left proud of the planking at 1 m (3ft 3in) intervals. The fifth to sixth

*5.5. Sewn plank fastenings on three 19th and 20th century Vietnamese boats, showing different ways of keeping fastenings within the planking to prevent them being damaged when boats took the ground. (after Manguin)*

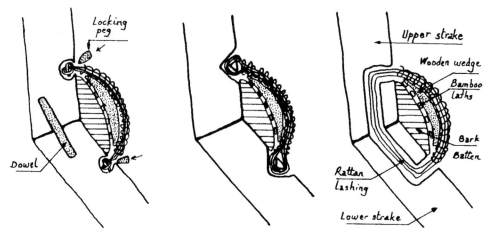

(?) century AD Khuan Lukpad boat (now in Wat Khpong Thom museum in south Thailand), and the fifth to seventh century AD planking of the Kolam Pinisi boat had similar features. Sewn-plank boats continued to be built in this region into recent times (Fig.5.5).

*Boats with treenailed planks*
The flush-laid planking (75 mm (3 in) thick) of several excavated boats from this region (ranging in date from the fifth/seventh to the eighteenth/nineteenth centuries AD) was fastened together by treenails (18 mm diameter) within the plank thickness. In the boats from Butuan in the Philippines, some treenails were locked in position by smaller treenails. All these vessels had cleats, integral with the planking, to which flexible framing timbers were lashed.

In 1988, eight planks (dated AD 610–775) from one vessel were recovered from the River Musi at Sambirejo, near Palembang in southern Sumatra. These planks, 14.5m long, of 35 mm average thickness, had been fastened together by treenails spaced at 18 cm, and by individual stitches of *ijok* (sugar palm – *Arenga pinnata*) spaced at c 76 cm. Cleats, to which framing timbers had formerly been attached, were at intervals of 0.50m. The relatively, closely-spaced treenail fastenings indicate that this was the primary means of fastening the planking together and the frames through cleats gave further support. The sewn fastenings were ancillary but may well have been essential since the treenails were unlocked.

*Ships with treenailed planks*
A fourteenth/fifteenth century wreck at Pattaya, off the Thailand coast, had bulkheads and three layers of planking – features that are sometimes taken to be typical of Chinese-built ships (see p.123–124, 126–127). Nevertheless, in contrast to the standard Chinese use of iron nails as plank fastenings, the Pattaya vessel's inner planking was fastened together by treenails, a South-East Asian characteristic. All plank scarves recorded were outboard of bulkheads; thus the inner planking of this vessel was not only fastened together but also fastened to bulkheads – a feature that is also found in fourteenth and fifteenth

century Chinese ships (see p.126). The inner planking of this Pattaya vessel was first fastened to that framework, and then fastened together. In other words, her hull shape was determined by her framing of bulkheads: that is, she was built 'framing-first'.

Other wrecks, similarly dated, fastened by treenails and with bulkheads, have been excavated: off the Vietnamese island of Phu Quoc (two) in the Gulf of Thailand and from Bukit Jakas, Pulau Bintan, in the Riau archipelago of Sumatra; from Malaysian waters: Royal Nanhai, Nanyasng and Laqqan; from the Philippines: Pandanan and Santa Cruz; and one from Hong Kong. Wrecks dated to later centuries and having bulkheads and treenail-fastened planking, but only one (or even no) outer layer of planking, have been excavated from the Gulf of Thailand: *Ko Si Chang 1 & 3*; *Ko Kradat*; and *Ko Khram*. Using the single criteria of having treenail plank fastenings, these wrecks are sometimes referred to as members of the 'South China Sea' tradition of shipbuilding, and are contrasted with wrecks that have iron plank fastenings which are likely to be Chinese (see p. 126–127).

*Boats with mortise and tenon fastenings*
In northern Vietnam, a first century BC, plank-extended logboat from Dong Xa, and second century AD planking re-used as a coffin lid at Yen Bac, were recently found to have locked mortise and tenon fastenings, as had undated wreck remains excavated in 1953 at Johore Lama, Malaya. These are all probably an outcome of BC/AD trading voyages to South-East Asia by ships of the Classical Mediterranean tradition. .

## CHANGES IN PLANKED BOAT AND SHIP BUILDING
Before the eighth century AD
The flush-laid planking of the earliest-known, South-East Asian boats was assembled using widely-spaced treenails within plank thicknesses, and then fastened together by individual lashings. These boats also had integral cleats (lugs) protruding from inboard planking surfaces, to which framing was lashed. Thus they have a general similarity with

the early, lashed plank Ferriby boats of north-west Europe (see Vol.1, p.109–112). Subsequently, the primary fastenings of the Sambirejo seventh/eighth century AD vessel were treenails, although she also had lashings between her flush-laid planks. From this time on, treenail plank fastenings have featured in every South-East Asian wreck excavated. Nevertheless, sewn planking was still used during the seventeenth to twentieth centuries in parts of this region – from Thailand to the Philippines and Malaya to the Moluccas.

### Eighth to fourteenth centuries
The typical vessel of this era had treenail-fastened planking with frames lashed to cleat-blocks integral with the planking. Again, this technique persisted into recent times in parts of this region: the Moluccan *orembai*; the Sea Dyak boats of Borneo; and the *prahu belang* of the Aru islands.

Outriggers appear to be another feature of this period: none has been excavated, but they are depicted on eighth/ninth century AD stone engravings at Borobudur in Java (Fig.5.2). During the sixteenth century, Europeans reported Moluccan fighting boats called *kora kora* that were notable for their stability and speed. These vessels had double outriggers on which were stationed, near-awash, rows of paddlers (up to 100 each side, it was said); marines manned the central, raised platform. Such vessels were probably in use from the eighth century or earlier.

### The fourteenth century and later
Thirteen vessels, excavated in South-East Asian waters and dated from the fourteenth to the seventeenth centuries (see p.99–100), were seagoing, round-hulled, cargo ships with keels, and some 20 to 25 m in overall length. They had flush-laid, primary planking fastened together by treenails and, with one possible exception, had a second (sometimes a third) planking layer. Moreover, those with substantial remains had bulkheads with associated framing, to which this planking was nailed. Since, in four of those finds (*Pattaya, Phu Quoc, Ko Si Chang 3* and *Bukit Jakas* of the fourteenth to sixteenth century), all,

or 'most', of the scarfs in their primary planking were outboard of bulkheads, it seems likely that they had been built 'bulkhead-first' (more generally, 'framing-first').

## PROPULSION AND STEERING

Apart from a side rudder found with the seventh/eighth century AD Sambirejo wreck from south Sumatra, and a number of mast steps in fourteenth to seventeenth century wrecks, evidence for propulsion methods and steering arrangements comes from documentary and iconographic sources.

A third century AD Chinese monk, Wan Chen, noted that large, seagoing South-East Asian ships had sails woven from the leaves of the *lu-thou* tree, that were 'obliquely set on four masts in a row from bow to stern'. One of the vessels depicted on sixth to seventh century frescos in Cave 2 at Ajanta, India has side rudders and is therefore thought to represent a South-East Asian vessel. This ship has a square sail on her bowsprit and high-aspect ratio sails (lugsails?) on three other masts. On the eighth/ninth century Buddhist temple at Borobudur, Java, eleven vessels are depicted: five (rafts) have outriggers and are propelled by canted, rectangular sails set on two bipod (possibly tripod) masts and a square sail on a bowsprit: they are steered by rudders on both quarters (Fig.5.2). Others, without outriggers, have a lugsail-type sail, set on a single mast.

The main ship represented on twelfth century reliefs at Angkor Thom in Cambodia has features that make it difficult to decide whether she was 'Chinese' or 'South-East Asian': her sails appear to be battened lugsails (Chinese) and some identify her rudder as a median one (Chinese): yet others see this as a rudder on the starboard quarter (South-East Asian).

South-East Asian *kora kora* fighting vessels were generally propelled by paddles, although occasionally sails of sackcloth and matting were set. Other representational evidence suggests that fore and aft sails set on two or more masts were used by South-East Asian ships from the third century AD, or earlier. The canted rectangular sail was in use by the eighth/ninth centuries and was widely used up to recent times. On the other hand, the battened lugsail seems to have been used, almost exclusively by the Chinese, from the twelfth century.

The median rudder was used in China from the first century AD; steering sweeps were also known from early times. Some of the boats depicted on the Dong Son drums of the first century AD (from sites in south-east China and, widely, from north-east Thailand to south-east Borneo) appear to have steering paddles or quarter rudders. A side rudder excavated from Sambirejo in south Sumatra is considered to be from the seventh/eighth century AD. Other evidence suggests that although paired quarter rudders may have been characteristic of South-East Asian ships in the sixteenth century, there may subsequently have been a degree of interchange of ideas about steering arrangements, between South-East Asian and Chinese shipbuilders.

Foil-shaped boards (*guares*), thrust down below the bottom of a boat or raft, can be used to steer a vessel by varying the number and position of foils and their individual immersed areas. Such devices are also used to oppose leeway and, today, they are found on sailing, rather than paddled or oared, craft. In Vietnam, they are used on basket boats as well as on log rafts (see p.94–96), but elsewhere (southern India, southern China and Central America – (see p. 54, 109–110, 165–166) they were, and are, predominantly used on sailing log-rafts. On at least one of the eighth/ninth century depictions at Borobudur, a *guares* seems to be used – a plausible interpretation since those depictions appear to be of raft-like vessels rather than boats (see p.93–94).

It is not yet possible to distinguish Chinese-built ships from South-East Asian-built ships, solely by their steering and propulsion arrangements.

## SOUTH-EAST ASIAN AND CHINESE SHIPBUILDING

Some of the structural features of medieval ships excavated from Chinese waters (p.120–127) are similar to those of their South- East Asian contemporaries. One distinctive difference is that treenails were used to fasten the primary planking of vessel built in South-East Asia, whereas, in China, angled metal nails were used (the fourteenth century *Penglai 1* ship – excavated from Chinese waters – is an exception to this rule as she has treenailed plank fastenings as well as metal spikes). Two other features may, in due course, enable us to differentiate ships from these two regions:

- a median rudder on Chinese ships; twin side rudders on South-East Asian ships;
- the battened lugsail may have been a Chinese characteristic, whereas in South-East Asia, the canted rectangular sail may have been dominant.

It might be thought that the bulkhead was a Chinese invention subsequently taken up in South-East Asia, since the earliest-known bulkheads were found on a seventh to ninth century wreck from Ju-kao, in the Chinese province of Jiangsu. Nevertheless, the eighth century author, Hui-Lin, states that South-East Asian ships were 'divided fore and aft into three sections' which may be a reference to bulkheads. Moreover, although the earliest wreck with multi-layer planking is dated to thirteenth century China, Hui Lin also states that the seagoing ships of South-East were built 'by assembling (several) thicknesses of side-planks'. Bulkhead-strengthening devices and plank scarfs outboard of bulkheads (characteristics that indicate vessels were built framing-first) appear at about the same time in wrecks excavated from South-East Asian and Chinese waters: when wrecked, those vessels were not necessarily in their home waters. It is not yet possible to decide where such innovations originated (see p.126–127).

# CHAPTER 6

# China

C hina's topographical features have had a strong influence on her communication links with the rest of the world. The core of China is a relatively low-lying area extending *c.* 1,000 miles from the coast between the Gulf of Chichli (Bo Hai) in the north, and the Gulf of Tonking in the south. Within this region are three great rivers: The Yellow River (Huang Ho) in the north; then the Yangtze (Chang Jiang = long river); and the smaller Pearl River (Xe Jiang) in the south. These rivers, and the coast, form a water transport network that underpins the economy (Fig.6.1).

Outer China is a highland zone lying in a semi-circle from Manchuria in the north-east through Gobi and Mongolia to the mountains and jungles of eastern Burma and northern Indo-China. Unlike rivers in Inner China, those in Outer China either flow out of China or, being headwaters, can only be used with difficulty. The general inhospitable nature of Outer China effectively cuts off Inner China from contact with the rest of Asia, the only practicable way to the West being the hazardous and difficult caravan route known as the Silk Road. China's best outlet to the world has therefore always been by sea: across the Yellow Sea to Korea and Japan; by the East China Sea to Taiwan and the Ryukyu islands; and by the South China Sea to maritime South-East Asia, thence to India and beyond.

There is also a geographical division between North and South at a latitude of *c.* 35°N, north of the Yangtze. To the north, the upper reaches of the Yellow River flow through the yellow earth (loess) which leads to general fluvial instability in the region. In the second Millennium BC, this river entered the sea at the northern end of the Gulf of Chihli. By the thirteenth/fourteenth centuries AD it had moved

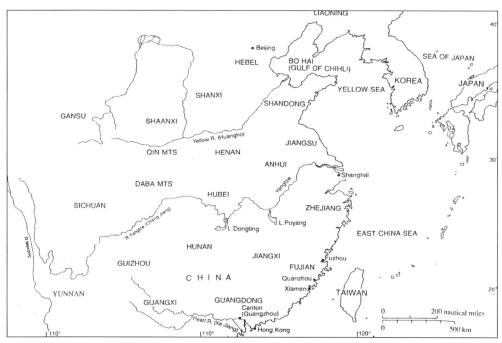

6.1. *Map of China showing the coastline, the main rivers and the principal provinces.*

southwards so that it entered the Yellow Sea south of the Shandong peninsula. In recent centuries it has moved north and south in an irregular fashion. The Yangtze and the Pearl, further south, are more stable. The Pearl with its tributaries forms a very fertile delta where it enters the South China Sea. The region between the Yangtze and the Pearl is crossed by other rivers, resulting in extensive and intensive use of water transport.

## CHINESE COASTAL WATERS.

In the summer, from May to September, the predominant wind in Chinese coastal waters is from the south, and typhoons, with storm-force winds, occur mainly in June to August. In the winter months, October to March, a seasonal, northerly monsoon wind prevails in both the Yellow and the South China Seas; in the East China Sea there are north-east trade winds.

Two main sea currents – one warm, one cold – affect the area. The Black current forms in the Malacca strait and flows northwards at *c.* 1.5 knots as a warm thirty nautical miles wide, stream, along the coast to the Korean

106

strait (between Korea and Japan), and on to the Japanese archipelago. The Lima (cold) current forms in the Tartar strait, between the Russian mainland and the Sakhalm islands, and flows southward along the east coast of Korea to enter the East China Sea near the Jizhou peninsula.

The best time for a southerly passage along China's coast is thus between October and March when there is a fair wind, albeit a foul current. In the early fifteenth century successive Chinese fleets, under the command of the Grand Eunuch, Zheng He, on a series of seven voyages to South-East Asia, the Indian Ocean and beyond (see p.125), timed their departure from northern ports so that the fleet was in coastal waters by January or February. Moreover, the admiral timed his return so that he was again in those coastal waters by July when there would have been fair, southerly winds and a north-flowing current, and the fleet would have been ahead of the main typhoon season.

In the northern sector of coastal waters (the Yellow Sea region, as far south as Hangzhou Bay at $30°$ N) river mouths and coastal seas are shallow, often with shifting sand banks. In the southern sector, in the East China Sea and the South China Sea, the rockbound coast has deeper water with offshore islands and fjord-like harbours. By the nineteenth century, two types of planked vessel appear to have been developed in those different regions, with differences that may well have arisen because of the coastal geography.

## NORTHERN AND SOUTHERN SHIP TYPES
In the late nineteenth and early twentieth centuries, northern and southern Chinese seagoing craft had much in common:

| | |
|---|---|
| Form: | Fore-and aft rocker. A transom stern and, above the waterline, a smaller transom bow. |
| Structure: | Built in the frame-first (bulkhead-first) sequence (bottom planking; bulkheads; side planking), but with the planking also edge-fastened together. |
| Propulsion: | Multiple masts and battened lugsails with multiple sheets. Leeboards fitted, especially in the north. |
| Steering: | Median (hoistable) rudder within a well. |

The differences between northern and southern types were partly structural but mainly in hull shape. The northern ship had a keel-less, flat bottom with a sharp chine, bluff, stem-less bows, and an overhanging stern. The southern ship was generally bigger with deeper draft and greater waterline beam. She had a keel, a v-shaped lower hull with rounded bilges and a sharper entry, and a more rounded stern. In general, her hull was more finely moulded and curvaceous than the northern type. The northern ship was clearly better for coastal and estuary work and, in particular, could take the ground well within tidal harbours. The southern ship, on the other hand, was more suitable for overseas voyages. It may be that these two different styles of ship were descendants of vessels built in earlier times.

**EARLY WATER TRANSPORT**
In addition to planked boats and ships, a wide range of floats, rafts and boats has been used in China during the recent past: floats of all types (Fig.6.2); bundle rafts, buoyed rafts and log rafts; and hide boats, bark boats and log boats. With the exception of fishing log rafts used off the coasts of Fujian Province, all were used in Outer China: in all likelihood, Inner China formerly had a similar range.

Bundle rafts
These had an unusual form in that the reed bundles were fastened at right angles to one another, making an open framework. There is a third century BC bronze bell with an engraving that may be of such a raft.

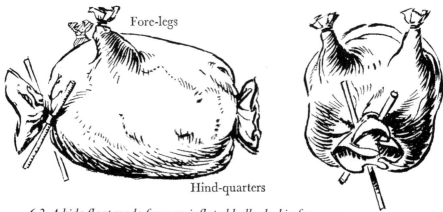

*6.2. A hide float made from an inflated bullock skin for use on the Huang Ho (Yellow River).*

Buoyed rafts

Rafts buoyed by hide floats were used to cross the Yellow river in the Han dynasty (206 BC–AD 220), and there are illustrations of them from the Ming dynasty (AD 1379–1644). Today they are restricted to the upper reaches of the Yellow River. Worcester noted that, after a passage downstream, the framework of such rafts was sold and the floats returned upstream (see p.33).

Log rafts

The earliest reference to a log or bamboo raft is from *c.* 472 BC, though Confucius (551–479 BC) is said to have used them. In recent centuries such rafts have been propelled by oarsmen on rivers (Fig.6.3); in estuaries, and off the Fujian coast, they were sailed (Fig.6.4). They are made from a dozen or so bamboos lashed together and to curved transverse bamboos, and those with sail are propelled by a balanced, mat lugsail on a single mast, in conjunction with two *guares* (see p.54, 94–6, 103, 165–166). Two steering oars over the stern further reduce leeway when close-hauled.

*6.3. A simple, one-man bamboo raft in use in sheltered waters.*

## Hide Boats

Hide boats are unknown in Inner China, but are used today on the headwaters of the Yangtze, Yellow, Yalung/Brahmaputra, Heilung/Amur, and in Korea. Rectangular boats are known in Tibet, the others are circular. There are references to their use from the fourth century AD onwards, and they were probably used by invading Mongols in the fourteenth century.

## Bark Boats

Bark boats have been reported on the River Amur in China's Manchurian province of Heilongjiang. It is also possible that they were used in Japan.

## Logboats

Contrary to Professor Needham's assertion, logboats have been widely used in China: moreover, they are used today in Outer China. Thirty to forty logboats have been excavated from the eastern and southern coastal provinces, but this is unlikely to be a complete distribution picture since they were exposed during development of the rivers' lower reaches. Two of those logboats have been dated by radiocarbon, others by stratigraphy or by association: the dates range from *c.* 4250 BC through to AD 618–909. Twenty or so log coffins, dated to before 221 BC, have been excavated in Sichuan and Fujian provinces: they are similar in shape to logboats, but have a partly-hollowed, half-log for a lid. Logboats have also been found in Japan, Korea and the Ryuku islands. Simple logboats are still used for fishing in the north of Japan and in Kagoshima Wan in the south.

Complex logboats, from earlier times and today, have been found in China, Japan and Korea. As in other parts of the world, Chinese boatwrights used a range of woodworking and boatbuilding techniques to increase the capacity and/or stability of the simple logboat: washstrakes were added to increasing height of sides; length was increased by the addition of a separate bow or stern; and the effective beam increased (hence increasing stability) by fitting stabilisers to a single logboat or by pairing two logboats; alternatively, bottom

*6.4. Model of a Taiwanese (Formosan) log raft with a matted lug sail. (National Maritime Museum, Greenwich)*

planking was inserted between the sides of a logboat that had been split longitudinally.

## Planked boats

The simplest form of planked boat is the tub boat: these are oval in shape, up to 8 ft long, 4 ft broad and 2 ft deep. They are built barrel fashion – short staves bound together by rope or by iron hoops (Fig.6.5) – are propelled by paddles and are used widely for river travel and fishing.

Pictorial characters, engraved on bone and on tortoise shell, and dated to the late-second Millennium BC, represent the oldest-known, Chinese word for 'boat' (Fig.6.6). This element is also contained within the

*6.5. A tub boat of the Yangste Jiang . After James Hornell, fig. 11 & plate xviii.*

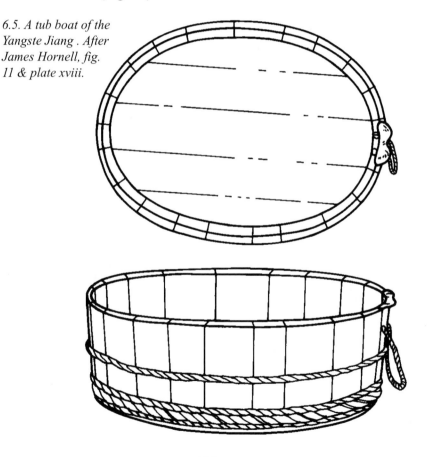

pictograms for 'ship', 'transport', 'caulk (or 'to sew') a seam' and for 'propel by oar'. There is also another, related pictogram which is considered to represent 'sail'. It has been argued by Professor Needham that the pictogram for 'boat' was originally derived from the shape and structure of the type of boat used in those days: a rectangular boat built of planks and with bulkheads – the traditional sampan!

### Sewn Plank Boats

There are no excavated example of Chinese sewn plank boat and very little representational or documentary evidence for them. They are,

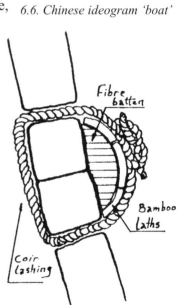

*6.6. Chinese ideogram 'boat'*

however, known to have been used in recent times in Outer China and adjacent lands: Japan, Thailand, Vietnam, Burma and Taiwan/Formosa and in Baoqing in Hunan Province. In the late-twentieth-century oared fishing boats with sewn planking were found by Dai on Hainan island in Guandong Province: their planking was fastened together with coconut-fibre rope, over a bamboo lath which held in place a caulking of cogon grass (Fig.6.7). Dai has also noted a text on plant life in southern China from the early fourth century AD stating that *gomuti* palm was used as boat's fastenings. In the twelfth/thirteenth century, Zhou Qufei recorded that large sailing ships were built in Guangdong province with sewn planking. There has evidently been a

*6.7 Sewn-plank fastening*

tradition of building sewn-plank boats in a region of southern China that may, in earlier times, have been culturally South-East Asian.

*Early excavated plank boats and models*

There are three excavated plank boats dated to the Han dynasty (second century BC to early third century AD): one is from Yanghe, Chuangsha Co. Shanghai; another from Wujin Co. Jiangsu; and the third is from Guangzhou: all three appear to be paddle-propelled, river boats. The Guangzhou boat seems to be a three-plank boat with rising ends; the other two are also three-plank boats but of an unusual construction: the central plank is, in effect, a thick plank-keel with a hollowed upper surface and a horizontal scarf towards one end; the two side planks are also slightly hollowed and fit into rabbets along the upper edges of the plank-keel: planking is said to have been nailed together. Horizontal holes at regular intervals near the upper edges of two side planks may be where crossbeams formerly fitted.

A fragmented, wooden tomb-model from Chuangsha of the first century BC, now in the National Historical Museum in Beijing, represents a punt-shaped, oared river boat. Oars are worked through ports in the sides, and a steering oar is pivoted within a notch at the stern. No framing is apparent and there is no indication of plank fastenings. A first century AD pottery model (Fig.6.8), now in the Guangzhou Museum, has a similar shape to the Chuangsha model. This pottery boat also has no visible framing and structural details are

*6.8. A 1ˢᵗ century AD pottery boat model from Guangzhou Museum. The boat has a median rudder (to the right) and an anchor is suspended from the bow (to left). (Guangzhou Museum)*

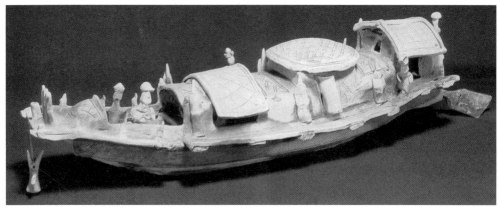

not depicted, but it has two hatchways giving entrance to the hold, and poling walkways each side. An anchor stone with wooden flukes is suspended from bollards in the bows. The boat was steered by a trapezium–shaped, balanced, axial rudder, slung under the overhanging stern, which could be raised and lowered within a well: this is the earliest evidence for the use of a centre-line rudder in China.

Early Propulsion, Steering and Anchoring

The model boat illustrated in Fig.6.8 has poling walkways; in the prototype, men would have walked aft along those walkways as they pushed on a pole to propel the boat forward. Sixteen model oars were found with a first century BC model from Chuangsha: they would have been pivoted through ports in the top strake, but it is not clear whether the oarsmen would have been seated or standing, nor whether they would have pushed or pulled their oars: today, Chinese working oarsmen frequently stand and push. A seventeenth-century account appears to be the earliest evidence for the *yuloh* (a sculling oar used over the stern), there is, however, a relief on a brick dated to the Han dynasty (206 BC to AD 220) that may depict a *yuloh* in use.

There is no direct evidence for early sail but ideograms on oracle bones and tortoise shell of the Shang dynasty (1529–1030 BC) have led Needham to suggest that sail was used before 1200 BC. The earliest description of a sail (in the *Shih Ming* dictionary of AD 100) and the earliest depiction (in the fifth/sixth century AD Buddhist temple at Chengdu, Sichuan Province) have convinced others that sail was first used in the Han dynasty, from the early second century BC. Early descriptions and depictions were evidently of a square sail. Professor Needham argued that southern Chinese ships had a fore-and-aft sail from the third century AD, but the text he quoted is ambiguous. Needham further believed that a ship depicted on the sixth/seventh century Ajanta frescos in India, and another depicted on the late-eighth century temple reliefs at Borobodur in Java, had lugsails: in neither case is it obvious that the vessels depicted are Chinese. Today, the battened lugsail is closely associated with Chinese sailing ships, but there is no firm evidence for such a sail until one is shown on a

Chinese ship carved in stone on the Bayon at Angkor Thom in Cambodia, and dated to *c*. AD 1185. On present evidence, the Chinese lugsail probably succeeded the square sail sometime in the early medieval period.

It has been claimed that the 'floating boards' on the Chinese vessel described in the late-eighth century *Tai Bei Yin Ching*, were leeboards, but leeboards do not float: this is more likely to be a description of stabilising timbers fastened to the ship and floating alongside the ship at the waterline, thereby increasing the vessel's transverse stability. The earliest undisputed reference to Chinese leeboards is from the seventeenth century. With a deep rudder, fore-and-aft sails and possibly leeboards, early medieval Chinese vessels could have had a reasonable windward performance, and claims for that have indeed been made by recent Chinese authors.

*Steering*
Steering sweeps over the stern, were used in China from at least the first century BC: they continued in use on river craft until the present century. The median rudder is first documented from the first century AD.

*Anchoring*
That first century AD model boat in Guangzhou Museum (Fig.6.8) has an anchor, with a stone stock and two wooden flukes, suspended from a bollard (or possibly a capstan) in the bows. Three stone stocks from a similarly constructed anchor, found near Quanzhou, have been dated to the twelfth and thirteenth centuries. A twelfth century account states that such an anchor would be suspended by a rattan rope from a windlass in the bows. As in other parts of the world, it seems likely that simple anchor stones would have preceded the use of anchors with stone stock and wooden flukes.

**LATER WATER TRANSPORT**
Iconographic Evidence
A carving on a fifth of sixth century AD stone stele in the Wan Fu Si

116

temple at Chengdu depicts what may be the earliest known representation of a Chinese coastal sailing ship. Sailing vessels depicted on seventh century frescos in the cave temple at Dunhuang may also have been similarly used: like the Chengdu ship, they have a single square sail set on a pole mast stepped well forward. They are also propelled by oars and are steered by oars on each quarter. One of several vessels depicted in the late-twelfth century Bayon Temple at Angkor Thom in Cambodia, is a keeled, planked vessel with a stem and an overhanging stern. She has two, matted and battened sails set with multiple sheets. At the stern she has a rudder extending below the keel and an anchor hanging from a windlass in the bows. Drawings of Chinese *jonqs* on the Catalan World Map of the late fourteenth century depict transom-ended vessels with five masts on which high aspect ratio (lug?) sails are set. A median rudder is set within a well in the after hull.

Documentary evidence

The Italian traveller, Marco Polo of the late thirteenth century, and Ibn Battutah, the Arab traveller and geographer of the mid fourteenth century, compiled accounts of their expeditions in the East which included comments on aspects of Chinese shipping.

Polo is believed to have lived in China from 1275 to 1292. He noted that, in the lower reaches of the Yangtze, there were countless log rafts and many ships that had one mast with a single sail and could carry the equivalent of 200 to 600 tonnes of cargo. These river ships were towed upstream (by boats or men?) using ropes of split bamboo.

Polo also saw large, seagoing ships in *Zaytun* (Quanzhou in Fujian Province): they generally had four masts, each with a single sail; two other masts could be stepped and rigged when needed. On windless days, or when manoeuvring in harbour, they were propelled by sweeps, each sweep being manned by four oarsmen. Polo noted that some of these ships had a draft of 4 paces (10 feet?).Their crew varied from less than 150 to more than 300: unless a good proportion of these were marines (see Ibn Battutah's account below) these numbers defy belief On the one deck below the weather deck, were up to 60 cabins for merchants – such 'cabins' were probably enclosed bunks, as in the twentieth century Antung trader. The hold was divided into thirteen compartments by planked bulkheads. Ships had double thickness pine or fir planking, caulked with *chu-nam*, and fastened together by iron nails. When ships had been at sea for a year or more, or needed repairs to the hull, a third layer of planking was fastened on top of the original double-thickness planking.

Polo noted that these ships could carry up to 6,000 'baskets of pepper' probably equivalent to *c.* 300 tonnes – this compares well with estimates of 200–250 tonnes for the cargo capacity of Quanzhou 1 (see p.120–126). The largest of these ships had two or three large boats and several smaller boats as tenders. The larger boats, under oars or sail, were used to tow the ship (on windless days and in harbour?); on passage they were themselves towed by the ship. The smaller boats were used for fishing and during anchoring; when on passage, they were lashed to the ship, outboard.

During his lengthy pilgrimage around the Muslim world, Ibn Battutah visited China in AD 1347. He noted three sizes of seagoing vessels: *jonq*, the largest with twelve sails; *zaw*, medium sized; and *kakam*, the smallest with three sails. Battutah considered Zayton (Quanzhou), with 100 large *jonq* and innumerable smaller vessels, to be the largest port known to him. The largest vessels were built only at Zayton and at Sin-Kilan/Sin al Sin (Guangzhou – formerly Canton).

Ibn Battutah's account gives details which suggest that the lower hull of a *jonq* was built 'plank first'. It is possible, but not certain, that the upper hull was then built 'frame-first'. Battutah tells us that the largest *jonq* had four decks, each with merchants' cabins, and was manned by 600 seamen and 400 marines – as with Polo, such large numbers are difficult to accept. Each *jonq* had four tenders of varying sizes. Sails were made of split bamboo matting. Sweeps were each manned by two men, one facing forward, one aft. The looms of the sweeps were too thick to be grasped and rope lanyards were fitted for oarsmen to pull. The twenty sweeps would have been positioned ten sweeps on each side, and manned on a deck just above the waterline.

If allowances are made for the exaggeration and ambiguities in Polo's and Battutah's accounts, it will be seen that there is a certain agreement between their descriptions of Chinese ships and the data recently acquired from a number of Chinese wrecks of approximately the same date, that were excavated during the late twentieth century (see Figs.6.10 and 6.11).

Excavated Medieval Vessels
Three T'ang period (seventh to ninth century AD) vessels have been briefly published. Of these, one excavated before 1961, from Rugao, Nanjing, was flat-bottomed with eight bulkheads nailed to the planking (or vice versa?); the hull was caulked with lime and tung oil. An apparently similar vessel (a 'junk') was documented by Admiral Pâris in the late nineteenth century (Fig.6.9).

In 1984 a small eleventh century vessel was excavated at Wando island off the south-west coast of Korea. A six-and-a-half metre length

*6.9. A small, 19th century Chinese vessel (a 'junk') in Macao – Admiral Pâris.*

of the bottom of this vessel and a 7.4m length of side planking were recovered, but not her ends or framing timbers. The three central strakes of this wreck were fastened together, edge-to-edge, by six transverse timbers that passed through the thickness of each plank, almost in raft fashion. The outer bottom strakes were fastened to the central strakes by six similar timbers that passed through the outer strakes, but only a short way into the inner strakes where they were locked by a vertical treenail. L-shaped transition or chine timbers were positioned within rabbets cut along the outer edge of both outer bottom strakes, and locked there by vertical treenails. The lowest side strakes fit into a rabbet cut into the upper edge of that chine strake and were fastened by treenails, as were succeeding side strakes: such rabbeted-lap planks give an onlooker the impression of being overlapping, clinker planking. Horizontal holes through some of these side strakes are where framing timbers had been fitted. Two vertical holes in the centre of the central bottom plank may be where a mast was formerly stepped.

While this eleventh-century cargo ship does not display all the characteristics of the medieval Chinese seagoing vessel, she does have some of the diagnostic features: rabbeted-lap side planking and angular-driven fastenings through lapped planking. It seems appropriate, therefore, to consider this ship as a fore-runner of the Medieval Chinese tradition.

*Wrecks from the 13th–15th centuries*
Between 1974 and 1984, four medieval wrecks of seagoing ships were excavated in Chinese waters: two others – one excavated in Korean, and one in Indonesian, waters – were probably built in China.

*Quanzhou 1.*   Houhzou harbour in Quanzhou, South China. Dated *c.* AD 1277. Now in Ship Museum, Quanzhou (Fig.6.10; 6.11).

*Quanzhou 2.*   Fashi, in the River Jinjiang, south-east of Quanzhou, South China. Dated twelfth/thirteenth centuries. Now in Ship Museum, Quanzhou.

2

Freepost Plus RTKE-RGRJ-KTTX
Pen & Sword Books Ltd
47 Church Street
BARNSLEY
S70 2AS

# DISCOVER MORE ABOUT MILITARY HISTORY

**Pen & Sword Books** have over 4000 books currently available, our imprints include; Aviation, Naval, Military, Archaeology, Transport, Frontline, Seaforth and the Battleground series, and we cover all periods of history on land, sea and air.

Keep up to date with our new releases by completing and returning the form below (no stamp required if posting in the UK).

Alternatively, if you have access to the internet, please complete your details online via our website at **www.pen-and-sword.co.uk.**

**All those subscribing to our mailing list via our website will receive a free e-book,** *Mosquito Missions* by Martin W Bowman. Please enter code number ACC1 when subscribing to receive your free e-book.

Mr/Mrs/Ms ...................................................................................................

Address.........................................................................................................

.......................................................................................................................

Postcode..................... Email address....................................................

**Stay in touch:** facebook.com/penandswordbooks or follow us on Twitter @penswordbooks

**Website:** www.pen-and-sword.co.uk **Email:** enquiries@pen-and-sword.co.uk
**Telephone:** 01226 734555 **Fax:** 01226 734438

*6.10. Quanzhou ship 1 during excavation in 1974. (Quanzhou Museum)*

*6.11. Quanzhou ship 1 displayed in the museum. Note the bulkheads with their adjoining floor timbers, and the mast step timber to the left.*

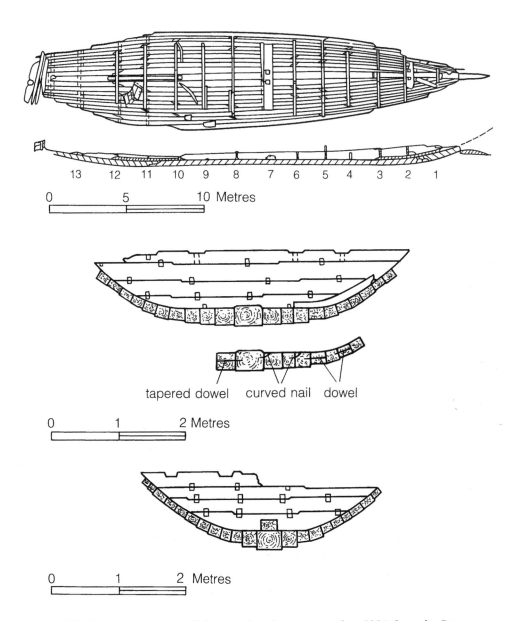

6.12. Plan and sections of the Penglai ship excavated in 1984 from the River Huahe in Shandong Province. Note that all plank ends (marked by a diagonal line on the plan) are at bulkhead stations. (after Xi & Xin)

| *Ningbo.* | Ningbo, Zhejiang, South China. Dated tenth to thirteenth century. |
| *Shinan.* | Shinan district, south-west coast of Korea. Dated. AD 1323. Timber species suggest she was built in China. |
| *Penglai 1* | Mouth of River Huahe, off Port Dengzhou, North China. Dated before AD 1376. Timber species suggest she was built in South China (Fig.6.12) |
| *Bakau* | Between Sumatra and Borneo. Dated *c.*1400. Bulkheads with 'stiffeners'and iron nailed planking with *chu-nam* caulking suggest that that this vessel may have been built in China. |

The first five wrecks were published in the Chinese language, although articles in English on three of them (*Quanzhou 1*, *Shinan* and *Penglai*) appear to present most (all?) details. It is possible to compile from the six wrecks a preliminary definition of the medieval Chinese, seagoing ship tradition:

*Form.* Underwater, these ships had a relatively sharp bow and a transom-shaped stern. Above the waterline they were more symmetrical with a transom-shaped bow above the fore-stem. Transversely, they had a generally rounded bottom with flaring sides. Longitudinally, there was an angular, rather than a smooth, transitions between fore-stem and keel, and between keel and transom stern. High in the stern, there was a transverse superstructure that projected aft of the transom.

*Structure.* These vessels were ships with decks, with all that implies for structural strength. Two-part keels were joined together, and to the lower stem, by, horizontal scarfs, either half-laps or hooked. The after-keel was angled upwards at *c.*10° to the main keel, the lower stem was at *c.* 20° to the main-keel. Planks within strakes were joined at bulkhead stations in horizontal scarfs that were half-laps or hooked.

Strakes were generally edge-joined together in half-laps or rabbeted laps fastened by angled nails. The Penglai ship, on the other hand, had long, dowel/ treenail fastenings, as well as angled nails. Individually, neither of these strake fastenings was 'positive', as were the locked mortise and tenon fastenings of Classical Mediterranean ships and the clenched nail fastenings of medieval north-west European ships. Nevertheless, having two types of fastenings in the Penglai ship may well have been as effective. Moreover, this ship's planking was also fastened to her bulkheads.

The framework consisted principally of half-frames and associated bulkheads (with limber holes) which were spaced along the length of the vessel, at intervals which varied from *c.* 1.5m to 3m. Planking was fastened to the framework by nails driven from outboard. In addition, frames and bulkheads were nailed together, and the primary planking was further fastened to bulkheads by *ju* nails (*gua-ju*), metal brackets (Fig.6.13), or by a wooden equivalent, hooked to the outer face of the planking, or jammed within its thickness. The second and third layers of planking in Quanzhou 1 (Fig.6.14) were secondary structure, although they strengthened the hull and enhanced its integrity. It may be that, as Marco Polo had reported was done in his day, the third layer was a reinforcement added (around the waterline?) during the vessel's working life, to increase transverse stability. The builders of these ships, as their predecessors had done at the time of Marco Polo, caulked planking with *chu-nam*, a putty made of jute fibre, shredded bamboo, lime and tung tree oil. This mixture was also used to seal the heads of planking nails, thereby minimizing corrosion. Irregularities in the plank surfaces were filled by a similar putty, but without fibre.

*Building Sequence.* The strakes of the *Quanzhou 1* and *Penglai 1* ships were edge-fastened yet their plank scarfs were (mostly/all?) at bulkhead stations (Fig.6.12). Furthermore, they had *ju* nails, or similar fastenings, between the planking and bulkheads that were so positioned that, in *Penglai 1*, the bulkheads were almost certainly in place before the planking was fitted. If this hypothesis is correct, the lower hull of *Penglai 1* was built in the frame-first (bulkhead-first) sequence: her hull shape was determined by her framework and not by the planking. It is likely that *Quanzhou 1* was similarly built.

A comparable change from the plank-first sequence of shipbuilding

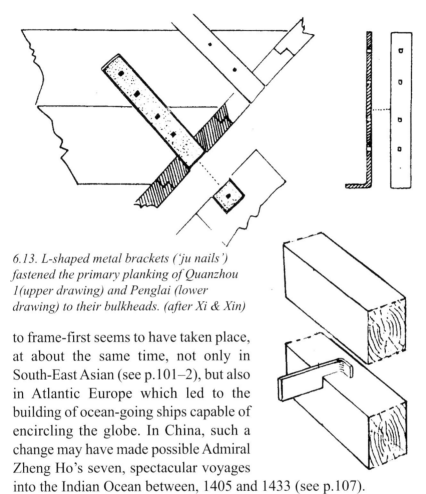

6.13. L-shaped metal brackets ('ju nails')
fastened the primary planking of Quanzhou
1(upper drawing) and Penglai (lower
drawing) to their bulkheads. (after Xi & Xin)

to frame-first seems to have taken place,
at about the same time, not only in
South-East Asian (see p.101–2), but also
in Atlantic Europe which led to the
building of ocean-going ships capable of
encircling the globe. In China, such a
change may have made possible Admiral
Zheng Ho's seven, spectacular voyages
into the Indian Ocean between, 1405 and 1433 (see p.107).

For the Penglai bulkheads to be used in this 'active' way, they
would probably have had to be fastened to the keel: whether this was
so, or not, is not mentioned in the published account. Other points that
remain to be clarified are: whether plank scarfs were fastened together
or merely fastened to bulkheads; the precise spacing of those
bulkheads, centre to centre; whether there are strake fastenings
immediately outboard of all bulkheads; whether all strakes were
fastened to all bulkheads; and whether caulking was inserted before
or after the planking was fastened.

Generally speaking, edge-fastened planking indicates that a hull was built plank-first, but there are exceptions to this 'rule' – see descriptions by Dr Greenhill and by Dr Coates. It is entirely practicable to fasten planking together with angled nails (Fig.6.13) or treenails *after* the strakes have been individually fastened to a bulkhead framework. Indeed, twentieth century Chinese junks were built in this manner. Moreover, boats of Gujarat in western India in the early twentieth century were built frame-first yet had edge-fastened planking (see p.61). As with certain medieval ships of South-East Asia (see p.101–102), until more information about these Chinese ships becomes available, it is not possible to confirm that they were built (and 'designed') bulkhead-first, although that seems to be highly likely.

*Propulsion and Steering.* Chinese seagoing ships had two masts, each stepped in a timber across the keel and lower planking: the foremast was 17-22 % of the ship's overall length from the bow; the main mast, 52-57 %. For sailing and steering balance, it may be that a third mast (a mizzen) would have been stepped further aft (possibly not on the keel). A near-vertical, median rudder was hung at the stern, positioned so that its stock could rotate within a groove in the stern transom.

Chinese and South-East Asian Shipbuilding (see p.103–4)
Similarities between the two traditions are striking. Both have:

- bulkheads with special fittings;
- (possibly) built bulkhead-first;
- multi-layer planking.

If the Penglai ship is excluded, there are four main differences between Chinese and South-East Asian medieval ships:

- Chinese: primary planking fastened by angled nails; South-East Asian: treenails.
- Chinese: median rudder; South-East Asian: twin side rudders.
- Chinese battened lugsail; South-East Asian: canted rectangular sail.

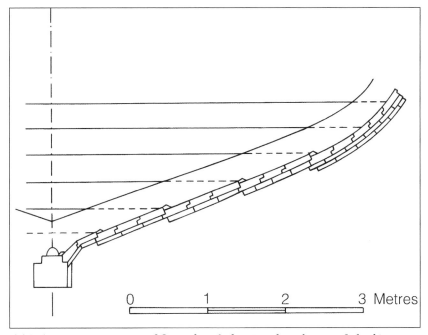

*6.14. A transverse section of Quanzhou 1 showing three layers of planking near the presumed waterline: the extra planking would have enhanced the ship's transverse stability. (Quanzhou Museum)*

- Chinese planking was caulked with *chu-nam* putty; this was not used in South-East Asian ships.

Medieval Chinese and South-East Asian shipbuilders seem to have become familiar with each other's techniques, facilitated by the overseas trade between them. Which way shipbuilding information flowed may become clearer as more medieval ships are excavated, documented, dated and provenanced. The identification of the timber species used in excavated ships, and dendrochronological data, should lead to the recognition of the region in which the vessel was built.

## PILOTAGE AND NAVIGATION

The change from environmental to instrumental navigation appears to have begun earlier in Chinese waters than in Europe. The properties of a magnetised needle seem to have been known in China from Han times (206 BC–AD200) and, by the medieval period, the azimuth plane of the compass was divided into 48 'points', each equal to 7½°. By the late thirteenth century, compass headings for certain destinations were recorded and, by the fourteenth century, compilations of such data were published. The earliest surviving chart is from the early Ming Dynasty (fifteenth century), but it is believed that they were first used at sea in the thirteenth century.

In a 'rutter' (pilot's handbook) that has survived from the fifteenth century, compass bearings for destinations in the South and West Oceans are given, and distances are given in 'watches' of 2.4 hours each. It is thought that, from the twelfth century, time was measured by burning calibrated incense sticks. Use of the 'Dutchman's log' was first noted in the third century AD: a log was thrown overboard and timed by 'running quickly to the stern'. Sand clocks may have been used at sea from the fourteenth century. Estimates of latitude on land, by measuring sun-shadow lengths, were being made in AD 724. By the sixteenth century, and possibly earlier, Chinese seamen used the Arab *kamal* to estimate, with some accuracy, latitudes in terms of Polaris altitudes.

CHAPTER 7

# Oceania

Oceania may be defined geographically as the islands of the southern Pacific and the adjacent seas to the west; in cultural/linguistic terms, these are the islands of Polynesia, Micronesia and eastern Melanesia (Fig.7.1). The Polynesian islands lie within a 4,000 miles-sided triangle, with its apices in Hawaii, Easter Island and New Zealand. If Hawaii and New Zealand are excluded, these islands appear to form an extension to the east-south-east of island South-East Asia. Micronesia with its 3,000 islands is east of the Philippines and north of Melanesia. Eastern Melanesia lies east-south-east of island South-East Asia and to the west of Polynesia; apart from Easter Island and Rapa at *c.* 25° south, and New Zealand at 35°– 45° south, Oceanic islands are generally within the Tropics. In longitude, they extend from 140°–160° east across the International Date Line to Easter island at 110° west, a mere 2,000 nautical miles from the west coast of South America.

## THE OCEANIC MIGRATION

The further east of the Solomons (*c.*160°E) that islands are, the smaller and more remote they tend to be. Moreover, the 200 nautical miles passage between the easternmost of the Solomon islands and the Santa Cruz islands, includes a long stretch out-of-sight of land. There is a similar stretch, further north, between the Philippines and the Micronesian islands to the east. These physical characteristics form a natural barrier to overseas expansion which probably explains why the migrants of 40,000 years ago (see p.78–82), did not continue further eastwards into Oceania.

A line drawn from east of the Solomons to east of the Philippines

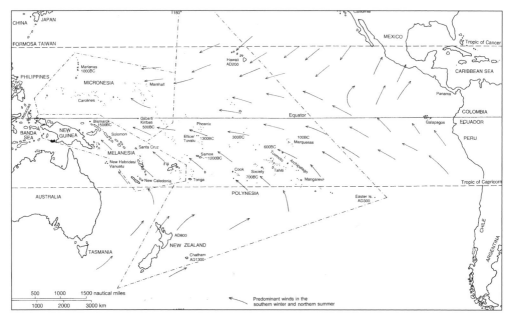

*7.1. Map of Oceania showing its many archipelagos and the winds that predominate during the southern winter/northern summer.*

(Fig.7.2) would separate 'Near Oceania', to the west, from 'Remote Oceania' (eastern Melanesia, Micronesia and Polynesia), to the east. Before exploratory voyages into Remote Oceania could be considered, voyage tactics had to be revised, methods of navigation out-of-sight of land developed, and boats had to be conceived and built that were not only capable of longer overseas passages, but also were able to carry plants and animals as well as people.

Although islands generally decrease in size and increase in remoteness, from west to east, there are many groups of islands clustered together in archipelagos, with intervisibility between islands within each group – for example: Fiji in eastern Melanesia; the Carolines in Micronesia; and Tonga in the west, and the Tuamotus in the east, of Polynesia. This feature simplified the problems of discovery and settlement since these groups not only formed a larger target for reconnaissance probes and were a 'safety net' for subsequent voyages further east, but also allowed several islands to be investigated on one exploratory voyage. Since voyages between island groups had evidently become much longer than could prudently be undertaken using paddles, it is likely that exploratory voyages were not considered until another form of propulsion could be used: the ability to sail seems to have been acquired by the mid second Millennium BC (see p.151–152).

The predominant winds in the southern winter/ northern summer are generally from the sector south-east to east-south-east over most of the region east of the Solomons, and generally east-south-east to east-north-east in Micronesia. In the southern summer the north-east trades blow in Micronesian waters, while there are generally south-east to east winds in the far west. The predominant winds were thus easterly (Fig.7.1), but with seasonal and regional variation: in the Bismarck/Solomon region there was a 50–70 % chance in the southern summer of monsoonal westerlies; around the tropic of Capricorn, from New Caledonia to Easter island, there was a 30–50 % chance of westerlies in winter; nearer the Equator, as far as central

*7.2. Map with a pecked line distinguishing Near Oceania from Remote Oceania. To the east of that line, archipelagos are more widely spaced than in Near Oceania. (after Ambrose)*

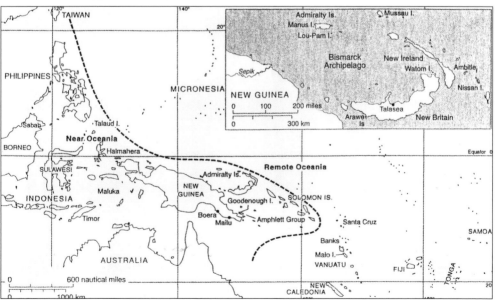

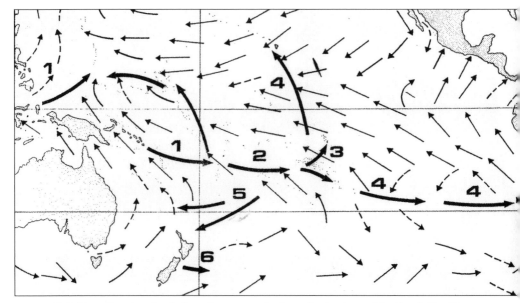

*7.3. Map showing the deduced sequence in the colonisation of the South Pacific. (after Irwin, 1992)*

Polynesia, the chance of westerlies was greater in summer; furthermore, outside the doldrums, there was a 15–25% chance of westerlies throughout the year.

In the light of linguistic, biological and archaeological evidence, it is now generally agreed that settlers came from the west (South-East Asia and Near Oceania). A distinctive style of mid-second Millenium BC pottery, known as 'Lapita', first identified in the Bismark archipelago, has become a prime characteristic for recognising the earliest settlements in eastern Melanesia and western Polynesia. The general settlement pattern (Fig.7.3) further east, beyond this Lapita culture zone – mainly derived from radiocarbon dates – seems to have been:

Polynesia    1,000 BC–500 BC. From Fiji/Tonga to Samoa and Cook.

500 BC–BC/AD.    From Cook to Society, Tuamoto and Marquesas

| | | |
|---|---|---|
| | BC/AD–AD 750. | From Cook/Society or Marquesas to Easter; and from Tahiti and Marquesas to Hawaii |
| | By AD 1200 | From Cook/Society to New Zealand |
| | By AD 1500 | From New Zealand to Chatham |
| Micronesia | 1,000 BC–BC/AD | From Philippines/E.Indonesia to Marianas & Carolines |
| | BC/AD–AD 500 | From E. Melanesia/W. Polynesia to E. Micronesia |

## WATER TRANSPORT

Excavated boats

In 1973–1982, during the excavation of waterlogged deposits near Faro on Huahine in the Society Islands, part of an outrigger boom, a 12 m mast, two logboat fragments and elements of two planks with lashing holes were encountered. These finds were interpreted as the remains of a paired hull boat dated to the eleventh to fifteenth century.

In late 2013, after a storm, a hollowed length of wood (6.68 x 0.85 m) was recovered at Anaweka on the north-western coast of South Island, New Zealand. The timber (subsequently dated to approximately AD1400) proved to be from one side of a logboat hull, with 'false' ribs and part of a stringer carved in the solid. Notches worked in that stringer were thought to be where crossbeams had been housed, while four holes in it were probably where side planking had been lashed into position and caulked with bark wads. A sea turtle (a documented Polynesian cultural symbol) had been carved near one end of this lengthy fragment. At the other end was a butt joint where a further section of hull had formerly been fastened. The investigators interpreted this find as the remains of either a paired-hull boat or a single-outrigger craft.

Early observation by Europeans

More early information about Oceanic water transport is found in accounts compiled by eighteenth and nineteenth century European

133

explorers. There are, however, special difficulties in the interpretation of such textual and iconographic evidence. Against the advantage that such descriptions and depictions were mostly complied by professional seamen, must be set the disadvantage that those seamen naturally compared the features of Oceanic boats with those of their own boats and ships, and it is not always clear whether such comparisons were precise or merely general. Moreover, most of those depictions are not measured drawings, and details of the rig are obscured. Furthermore, it seems likely that details taken from several boats have sometimes been combined in one drawing, and the use of perspective may well give a misleading impression of shapes, sizes and relationships. Doubtful features may also have been depicted: Hodges' painting of a scene in Matavai Bay, during Cook's second voyage, includes two Tahitian boats with transom sterns, a structural feature not otherwise mentioned or depicted in early Oceanic accounts. Could this have been an indigenous feature or merely a recent borrowing, or even an artist's mistake? These accounts and depictions must be subjected to criticism, before an accurate picture can be compiled of Oceanic water transport in the eighteenth/nineteenth century.

Floats and rafts
In the nineteenth century, broad, flat planks, hewn from a hardwood tree, were used as surf boards by the indigenous peoples of Easter Island and Hawaii, and bundle rafts were noted in Fiji and New Zealand. Maori rafts were made from bound bundles of bulrushes or flax: they varied in size from one-man, sit-astride rafts to boat-shaped ones made from five bundles. Fiji rafts consisted of two large bundles of bamboo poles lashed together. Only one type of buoyed raft is known to have been used in Oceania: boat-shaped, wooden rafts were given extra buoyancy from dry fern stems and roles of flax stalks packed against bottom and sides. Larger rafts had inflated bladders of bull kelp attached: they were used for inter-island passages of up to twelve nautical miles.

Europeans noted that log rafts were used widely in eastern Melanesia and Polynesia and occasionally in Micronesia. Some were given tapering ends using the logs' natural taper and by positioning longer logs centrally; others were rectangular. Logs in some rafts were directly lashed together, in others they were lashed to transverse timbers: in Mangareva, logs were linked together by hardwood timbers. In Santa Cruz, Admiral Pâris noted a raft with an outrigger. Other unusual rafts were seen in nineteenth century New Zealand that had two sets of two-tiered logs, each layer being pinned together and the two layers lashed together; the two sets were held three to five feet apart by three transverse poles. The crew manned the larger set and the smaller set acted as an outrigger float. Log rafts were poled in the shallows and paddled elsewhere; uniquely, Society Island rafts are said to have been propelled by kites. The log rafts of Mangareva, Tonga and Yap had sails: those of Mangareva were 40–50 ft (12–15 m) long, and carried twenty or so fighting men on raiding voyages of more than twenty-five nautical miles. In Micronesia and Polynesia, large blocks of stone and coral were transported by raft – less arduous than loading and unloading them over a boat's sides. Micronesia limestone discs, up to 12 ft in diameter, were transported by raft from Palau to Yap, a distance of 350 nautical miles.

Logboats
In the twentieth century, small, un-extended and un-expanded logboats were used to fish inshore waters in New Zealand, Hawaii, and the Society Islands. Since many types of Polynesian plank boats are logboat-based, it seems possible that, in earlier times, simple logboats were built on islands that had suitable trees or had access to driftwood logs. In the early twentieth Century, James Hornell noted that, in New Zealand, stone tools and fire were used to build such boats. After the chosen tree had been felled, the master shipwright (*tohuna*) used charcoal to draw the outline of the boat upon the log. In Hawaii, the *kahuna* also had a priestly function. After being soaked in freshwater for some days, boats were given a final shaping, transverse timbers were inserted between the sides to prevent deformation, and the hull surfaces were smoothed with coral.

Planked Boats
When Europeans first arrived in Oceania, they noted three, distinctive types of planked boat: the single-hull boat; the boat with a single outrigger; and the paired or double-hulled boat. Within each type there were differences, nevertheless, all Oceanic boats had some common characteristics:

- they were built plank-first, the planks being sewn together before the framing was fastened to them;
- in general terms, hulls were similar in structure and in shape;
- sails, although different in detail, were mainly variants of the triangular sail with its apex down.

Where large trees or drift logs were not available, boats were built entirely of planks with a conventional keel. On Easter Island, where suitable timber was especially in short supply, boats were built from planks that were only 4–5 in (10-13 cm) broad and 2–3 ft (60–90 cm) long. On islands that were well-endowed with timber, on the other hand, the lowest element of each boat was a hollowed log, sometimes in two or more sections: in essence, these were plank boats built on a logboat base.

*Boatbuilding tools and techniques*
Neolithic tools were used: trees were felled with stone axes and by controlled use of fire. The Maori of New Zealand used a swing battering ram to fell tough pine trees. Ingenious methods had evolved of moving logs to the building site, using five-stranded ropes made from the leaves of *Cordyline* species, rollers, skids, levers, wedges, handspikes and parbuckles. Wedges were also used to split planks from logs. Tools generally were of stone but blades were also made from sea snail and giant clam shells: all had to be sharpened frequently. Sharpened bones set in a wooden handle were used as gouges and, in conjunction with a wooden mallet, to make fastening holes. Hulls were smoothed with ray skins and sometimes given a final 'polish' with sandstone.

*7.4. Maori method of tightening sewn fastenings. Similar leverage procedures must have been devised wherever sewing was used to fasten planking. (after Best)*

To form a curved section, planks were hollowed rather than bent. Strakes were set either edge-to-edge or with a protruding lap joint; planks within strakes were end-butted. Admiral Pâris noted that the planking of Tuamoton boats was first held in position by treenails within the thickness of the planking before it was sewn together – this practice is known to have been used elsewhere, for example, in Egypt (see p.9), the Mediterranean (see Vol.1, p.79) and South-East Asia (see p.98). Generally in Oceania, strakes and scarfs were sewn together (Fig.7.4), sometimes through projections from the planking, sometimes through holes bored through the planking. A caulking of green coconut husk mixed with sticky, breadfruit gum was held in place by a longitudinal lath, and three-ply coconut fibre (*sennit*) was then used to sew the planks together. These boats had to be dismantled and re-sewn after three months seafaring.

### Single-hull boats
European explorers found three different versions of single-hull boats in New Zealand, Tonga, Tuamotu, and the Austral and Society islands:

- small boats, logboat-based, were used for fishing;

7.5. A late-20<sup>th</sup> century reconstruction (a 'floating hypothesis') of a small Maori war boat.

7.6. An early-20<sup>th</sup> century Polynesian sewn-plank boat at Vahitahi, in the Toamotu archipelago. This 24ft long, keeled boat was said to be 'one of the last voyaging canoes'.

- larger and more complex boats, logboat-based and sewn-planked, with a bow figurehead and a vertical stern – these were war boats, mostly paddled (Fig.7.5) but sometimes under sail;
- fully-planked and sewn, 'voyaging canoes', propelled by sail on a mast stepped well-forward, and with a steering oar (Fig.7.6).

*Double- hull boats*

European explorers noted that paired (double-hull) boats were used to display 'power and prestige', and sometimes actually for war. They were frequently seen in great 'fleets' – for example, 159 such boats, 50–90 ft (15–27 m) long, with a crew of fifty to 120 men. The two hulls, generally similar in shape and size, were positioned up to eight feet apart, and connected by transverse planks, beams or poles lashed to each hull. Above these timbers was a wooden platform upon which a matting shelter was sometimes erected. Linking two hulls, each with a waterline beam of 2–3 ft (60–90 cm), in this way, gave an effective beam of at least 12 ft (3.7m), with a consequent marked increase in stability, a wider baseline for the rigging, and more space for people and gear.

Paired boats with hulls of (near) equal length were given a definite bow and stern, by stepping the mast forward of amidships; generally, this mast was in the starboard hull but, in Hawaii, it was between the hulls. Such craft were tacked by steering the boat through the wind. In the seventeenth/early-eighteenth century, these boats were seen in Santa Cruz, Tonga (Fig.7.7), Hawaii, Tahiti and New Zealand.

In late-eighteenth century eastern Melanesia, and throughout Polynesia, paired boats had unequal hulls, the shorter hull being some 65–80% the length of the main hull, with the mast stepped near amidships (occasionally, two masts were noted). When required to change tack, such craft were 'shunted': that is, the end that was the 'bow' on one tack became the stern on the next tack; the rudder was moved from one end to the other, and the mast and sail adjusted to match the new configuration.

*7.7. An early-17$^{th}$ century, double-hull/paired boat being pursued off Tonga. (after Haddon & Hornell)*

## Boats with outriggers

The boat featured frequently in early European reports from Oceania was the one with a single outrigger. Those boats were generally very narrow in relation to their length and depth of hull: typical dimensions are 11.5 x 0.8 x 1.10 m, giving L/B = 14; L/D = 10.5. Such slim, lightweight craft have high-speed potential, an attribute that in a conventional boat would be accompanied by limited transverse stability, but, in this case, the outrigger confers adequate stability with only a slight increase in resistance to motion. The float, a simple wooden cylinder or of a more complex shape, was positioned some one-third of the boat's waterline length away from the hull, at the end of a boom fastened to the boat's framing. Such outrigger assemblages were configured so that, with the boat in an upright condition, the float was close to the water and stabilised the boat transversely.

Some outrigger boats were double-ended, either end being used as the bow: these boats had their single mast stepped either amidships or towards the bow, the aim being to obtain sail balance. Other vessels had a definite bow and stern, with the outrigger usually to port and their single mast invariably stepped towards the bow. The position of the mast step determined how these boats were handled when changing heading relative to the wind. With the mast forward, the boat was tacked through the wind, the outrigger being to windward on one tack and then to leeward. When the outrigger was to leeward, the helmsman's aim was to keep the float just submerged so that its buoyancy opposed the wind-induced heel.

In contradistinction, those boats with the mast stepped amidships were 'shunted': the rudder was moved from end to end, making the bow become the stern, the sail was adjusted to match the new configuration, and the new bow was then brought closer to the wind. On both tacks, the outrigger was to windward. In this condition, the aim was to keep the float skimming the water so that its weight counter-balanced the heel due to the wind.

There are a few illustrations of Oceanic 'mast-amidships' boats with an outrigger depicted to leeward. One, by de Bry shows several boats under oars and sail, off the Marianas: this is usually described as an 'artist's mistake'. Another, by Admiral Pâris (Fig.7.8), shows a vessel with its outrigger to leeward with the float submerged; three of her crew are on a windward platform to counteract the resultant list. Pâris explained that this boat had been taken aback, and he had depicted her when almost recovered. It thus seems that this vessel had

7.8. Two mid-19<sup>th</sup> century, single outrigger boats of the Caroline islands, each with a balance board. The boat to the right is recovering after being taken aback. (after Admiral Pâris)

indeed been sailing with her outrigger to leeward with float submerged to counteract the de-stabilising effect of the outrigger. It has been suggested that, although a 'mast-amidships' boat with her outrigger to leeward is less stable than when 'shunted' (when the outrigger is always to windward), having the outrigger to leeward may enable the boat to get closer to the wind.

The earliest-known single-outrigger boat in the Santa Cruz group of Eastern Melanesian islands, was double-ended, had her mast stepped amidships and her outrigger to windward with a lee platform on the opposite side: she was probably 'shunted'. Fine adjustments to transverse trim were made by stationing one of the crew on the lee platform/balance board.

Micronesian single-outrigger boats were seen in the Marianas in

1521, during Magallan's circumnavigation voyage: they were double-ended with a steering paddle at each end. Pigafetta, Magallan's chronicler, noted not only that either end of these boats could be used as the bow, but also that they had an asymmetric transverse section, being rounded on the outrigger side, but near-vertical on the other: such a transverse section would not only compensate for the effects of the outrigger, but also would reduce leeway. These boats were noted for their 'great swiftness' and became known as 'flying proas'. By the early nineteenth century, boats of this type in the Caroline and the Marshall islands were fitted with a lee platform: such 'permanent balance boards' gave a better lead to the rigging and some had a small cabin built thereon. In one of Admiral Pâris' drawings, a man standing on such a platform balances the float on the opposite side so that it is just clear of the water. It seems likely that these later vessels were shunted rather than tacked, and thus always had their outrigger float to windward.

Outrigger boats in the western parts of Polynesia differed from those used in the rest of that region. In Tonga, boats had a definite bow, the outrigger float was invariably to port, and masts were stepped forward of midships. When on a starboard tack (wind from the starboard side) it may have been possible to balance the boat by stationing men on a platform that projected out to starboard. In later centuries, Tongan boats were seen with a canted mast stepped amidships: these could have been shunted with the float always to windward, or they could have been tacked using the windward side of the protruding platform to balance the boat when the float was to leeward. Samoan outrigger boats had a vertical mast that was stepped amidships: they were tacked rather than shunted.

In central, eastern and northern Polynesia, on the other hand, outrigger boats were unequal-ended with the mast stepped forward, and the outrigger float was always to port. In Tahiti and the Marquesas, these boats were tacked: on the starboard tack, transverse stability was obtained by stationing crew on the balance board. By the early nineteenth century, a two-masted rig had been evolved.

## PROPULSION AND STEERING
### Paddle, pole and scull
Paddles – to European eyes, large and unwieldy – were widely used, both for propulsion (often in conjunction with sail) and steering. Steering paddles were 'of great length and extremely heavy'. In the shallows, boats were poled/punted. European–style oars were unknown in Oceania, but there was a form of 'sculling'. Standing upright and facing forward, scullers worked the 11–12 ft, oar-shaped sculls near-vertically, through holes in the platforms of paired boats and through gaps between hull and outrigger.

### Propulsion by sail
To form an individual sail, mats of *pandanus* or coconut-palm leaves were sewn together, sometimes across, and sometimes along, the sail's length. Ropes, made of plantain tree fibres, were used to fasten sails to yards. Rigging lines used to control sails were made of three or four strands of this plantain rope bound together.

Masts of boats that were tacked, rather than shunted, were stepped in a substantial timber that held them in a vertical position. This step was fastened to the forward outrigger or, in paired boats, to a forward crossbeam. In paired boats with two masts, both could be between the hulls or one would be port forward, the other starboard aft. Fijian double-ended boats were shunted and therefore needed the mast to be canted alternately towards one end then the other. To allow this, the notched heel of the mast was pivoted on a ridged chock that was lashed to the central outrigger boom or, in a paired boat, to a central crossbeam. Such masts were often further supported higher up by a shore with a fork at its lower end that pivoted about a boom or a beam.

Standing rigging was generally similar to that of European rigs. Masts were supported by stays and by shrouds that often were in pairs (sometimes as many as six or seven) and the shroud base was made as broad as possible using outriggers, lee platforms, balance boards and out-rigged balance spars. Running rigging was somewhat different. Generally, there were no sheets or reef points, and Anson considered that sails were reefed by rolling them around the boom. The effective

*7.9. A single-outrigger boat seen by Magallan in the Marianas in 1521.*

area of a triangular sail was varied by tricking up a spiller line running from the boom, via masthead or yard, to the deck, thereby bringing the boom closer to the yard. Cook considered that the sail of Tongan boats that tacked might be shifted to leeward after unlacing the lower part from the yard. In later years, Oceanic seaman followed the European practice of fitting a halyard so the yard and furled sail could be sent down.

*Oceanic sailing rigs.* (Fig.7.7, 7.8 & 7.9)
Europeans who first saw Oceanic sails marvelled at their distinctive shapes and their unusual rigging, and noted that, while some sails appeared to be set without a yard, all had a boom. The use of familiar European sail-names to describe them led to confusion since most, if not all, South Pacific sails had little resemblance to European sails. Over the years, attempts have been made to bring order and logic into the naming of these rigs but none has been successful. A further attempt is made here, based on the assumption that the most important variables are mast, yard and sail shape. Each rig so recognised is

identified by the place and date of the earliest reliable description
and/or illustration. Such an analysis leads to the recognition of six
types of Oceanic rig (Table 7.1).

**Table 7.1. Identification of early Oceanic sailing rigs**

| Type & date | Illustration | Variables |
|---|---|---|
| 1. Marianas, 1521 | BoW fig.9.11 | Canted mast, yard, triangular sail (Fig.7.9) |
| 2. Tonga, 1643 | H&H fig.187 | Vertical mast, yard, triangular sail (Fig.7.7) |
| 3. Tonga, 1777 | H&H fig.193 | Canted mast, yard, claw sail.(Fig.7.8) |
| 4. Tahiti, 1768. | H&H fig.77 | Vertical mast, no yard, half-claw sail |
| 5. New Zealand, 1769 | R&R fig.43 | Vertical mast, no yard, triangular sail |
| 6. Marquesas, 1774 | H&H fig.21A | Vertical mast, no yard, claw sail |

**Notes:**
BoW  =  McGrail, 2004. *Boats of the World*
H&H  =  Haddon & Hornell, 1936. *Canoes of Oceania.*
R&R  =  Rienits & Rienits, 1968. *Voyages of Captain Cook* – See also
         H&H, 1936: fig 141.

*Type 1 rig: Marianas, 1521.*   This sail was first documented by
Pigafetta in his illustration of Marianas, double-ended outrigger boat
seen during Magellan's expedition in 1521. Pigafetta described it as
'a lateen on an angled yard, in shape resembling a shoulder of mutton'.
The sails of outrigger boats of this region were subsequently seen to
be similar: these boats were shunted rather than tacked. This suggests
that Magellan's boat had a canted mast rather than the vertical one
depicted in what appears to be a diagrammatic or stylised illustration.
The preferred description is: 'a triangular sail with a yard set on a
canted mast'.

*Type 2 rig: Tonga, 1643.* First documented by Tasman at Namuka in Tonga in 1643. He noted that the mast of a double-ended, outrigger boat was short and vertical, and fitted well forward; the sail, triangular in shape, was laced to a curved yard resting in a masthead crutch at about its mid-point; the foot of the sail was fastened to a boom. Preferred description: 'a triangular sail with a yard, set on a vertical mast'.

*Type 3 rig: Tonga 1777.* Documented during Cook's third voyage on double-ended, outrigger boats, and on paired boats: the sail was suspended from a midship mast. Santa Cruz outrigger boats with lee platforms had a similar rig from the early nineteenth century. Such boats were probably shunted. Preferred description: 'a claw sail with a yard, set on a canted mast'.

*Type 4 rig: Tahiti 1768.* First documented on a Tahitian *va'a motu* outrigger boat, during Bougainville's 1768 voyage. The mast was stepped forward on such boats which were not double-ended but had balance boards: they were therefore tacked. Preferred description: 'a half-claw sail, without a yard, set on a vertical mast'.

*Type 5 rig: New Zealand, 1769.* First documented by Cook in 1769. These boats were not double-ended and would have been tacked. Preferred description: 'a triangular sail without a yard, set on vertical mast'.

*Type 6 rig: Marquesas, 1774.* First documented on outrigger boats during Cook's 1774 voyage. As the mast was stepped forward, these boats were tacked. Preferred description: 'a claw sail without a yard, set on a vertical mast'

Steering

Freely-held steering paddles ('like a baker's shovel') were used from the stern whenever possible, otherwise from the platform. In outrigger boats, steering paddles were used on the same side as the float. In boats that were shunted, paddles were fastened by long lanyard to the platform so that they could be floated from one end to the other.

## OCEAN-GOING CRAFT

Only insignificant remains of early Oceanic boats have been excavated, insufficient to deduce the shape of the original hull from them. Moreover, although 'reconstructed' vessels, such as Hokule'a, have been useful in testing non-instrumental methods of navigation, they can give only a general impression of the seafaring abilities of early-Oceanic crews and their boats. It therefore seems that assessments of such ability should primarily be based on the recorded observations of sixteenth to nineteenth century European seamen, and on conclusions drawn from recent ethnographic fieldwork.

### Speed

Doran has summarised early European comments on speeds achieved by Oceanic boats: Polynesian paired and outrigger boats were 'reasonably good'; Fijian paired boats and Micronesian outrigger boats were 'unusually fast'. One Fijian boat is said to have made twelve knots, and a Gilbertise 'flying proa' touched seventeen knots. Estimates given to Cook by Oceanic seamen, for longer distance passages under favourable conditions, were equivalent to 130–150 nautical miles a day. Lewis concluded that, with a fair wind, eighteenth to nineteenth century Polynesian double-hull, and Micronesian outrigger, boats could make 100–150 nautical miles a day – an average speed of four to six knots.

### Windward capability

There are no detailed European accounts of the windward performance of Oceanic boats. Dr Lewis has emphasised, however, that Oceanic seamen would have sailed 'full and by': sails full but not lifting or shaking, with moderate stress on boat and crew. In that 'full and by' state, he considered that Oceanic boats would have been seven points (75°–80°) off the wind.

## Capacity

Reports by Cook and other European seamen suggests that both outrigger and paired Oceanic boats of the eighteen and early nineteenth centuries would have been able to carry sufficient people and stores for a lengthy reconnaissance voyage. Moreover, it seems very likely that both types were structurally suitable for Oceanic voyages, and Polynesian and Micronesian crew of those days certainly had the necessary seafaring skills. However, outrigger boats of the eighteenth and nineteenth century would not have been large enough for settlement voyages when livestock, tools and utensils, and a greater number of people would have to be carried: paired boats or large outrigger boats would have been essential.

## Victuals

Dr Lewis noted that, in recent times, Oceanic seamen carried a variety of 'long-life' food to enable them to undertake lengthy sea passages: for example, *pandanus* fruit cooked, dried to form a paste and then wrapped in leaves could last up to two months. He concluded there would be no difficulty in provisioning a large boat for a month or even six weeks. Moreover, Cook had reported that the crew of Fijian paired boats burned coconut husks on a bed of sand, stone or clay on their platforms, and there cooked fish caught whilst underway. Water was carried in large bottle gourds, in coconuts or within bamboos.

Irwin has estimated that, on an ESE heading with a fair wind from the west, for every two, or even three, weeks on an outward passage, it would be safe to allow a week for a return with the predominant ESE wind. Assuming that early Polynesian reconnaissance boats could make 100 nautical miles a day, they would have had a safe radius of action of 1,500 to 2,000 nautical miles on an outbound passage of two or three weeks. In the event that no land was found, they would then have sufficient food for one week of a return passage with the predominant wind, leaving in reserve a fortnight on 'hard tack'.

## Which ocean-going craft?

Voyages east of the Bismark archipelago towards Polynesia, and from the Philippines into Micronesia, probably began *c.* 1,500 BC. Before such explorations could be undertaken, the proto-Polynesians and Micronesians had to learn how to sail and had to have developed ocean-going vessels of adequate capacity that could make good a track across the wind and thus not loose ground to leeward in the event of foul winds. Moreover, these explorers had to learn how to navigate when out of sight of land.

Rather than undertaking a single passage on which land would be both found and settled, it seems likely that the 'prudent Polynesian seaman' would initially undertake exploratory voyages, and, only after suitable land had been located, would a colonising passage be attempted. Thus two types of boat would be required: a reconnaissance craft, and one for migration with greater capacity and possibly having sea-kindly qualities. At first European encounter, there were four types of ocean-going craft in Oceania: the log raft and three forms of planked boat- the single-hull, the single outrigger and the paired-hull. It seems unlikely that the log raft would have been used in either of those roles, and the logboat-based, single-hull boats generally used in those times were not ocean-going.

Single-hull boats with a keel were used as 'voyaging canoes' in the nineteenth century, and possibly were so used in the ocean-going phase of Oceanic expansion. Nevertheless, it seems more likely that outrigger boats and paired-hull boats were used in those earlier times: the most developed of such boats, when first encountered by Europeans, were clearly capable of ocean voyaging. For reasons of speed and manoeuvrability, outrigger boats may well have been preferred for exploratory voyages, and paired-hull boats, with their greater capacity, for settlement passages.

With much conjecture, using evidence from the few boats excavated in South-East Asia, it is possible to compile a descriptive outline of an early Oceanic voyaging craft. Such a boat would have had sewn planking on a logboat base, the planking first being aligned and held in position by treenails within the plank thickness, then sewn together. Framing would then have been lashed to cleats integral with the planking. By 1500 BC, when the pre-Polynesians and the pre-

Micronesians were preparing to venture further eastwards, it may be that the sailing rig consisted of mast, yard and boom with a triangular sail set with apex down. This single mast may have been stepped forward of amidships and the vessel tacked through the wind. Steering would have been by sail balance, assisted by paddle. Leeway could have been reduced by the use of a large-bladed paddle.

## PASSAGES UNDER SAIL

From Figs 7.1 & 7.3, it can be seen that the main thrust of exploratory passages towards the islands of eastern Melanesia and Polynesia; and to Micronesia was on a heading of ESE i.e. into the predominant wind. Passages to these islands from the south, and passages from central Polynesia to Hawaii, would have been across that wind, while those to New Zealand were across, then into, wind. On headings against the predominant wind, sail would seem to have been impossible, but three further points must be considered:

- at a certain level of sailing development, boats can be sailed across the wind, and even make ground into wind. Could those Neolithic colonisers have acquired such skills by the mid second Millenium BC?;
- no seaman would sail on an exploratory voyage without being sure of a fair wind for his return passage. In AD 1492, Columbus used easterly winds to cross the Atlantic, knowing that, further north, he would find westerly winds for his return;
- predominant winds do not blow continuously.

In the light of their documented achievements, Oceanic sailors must be considered to have been competent, but not reckless, seamen who would not wantonly risk their lives. Professor Geoffrey Irwin of New Zealand, and others, have discussed how such seamen could have undertaken exploratory and settlement voyages. The generally agreed conclusion is based on the initial proposition that Oceania was systematically explored for new lands in the direction that gave the best chance of survival i.e. into the sector from which the predominant wind blew, but using non-predominant winds: whether or not new lands were sighted, when the predominant wind came to blow it would give them a safe and speedy return home. As sailing experience was gained, cross-wind passages to Micronesia and to Hawaii could have been undertaken; finally, New Zealand could have been discovered by vessels sailing out of the Tropics using the winds associated with travelling depressions.

Experimental voyages

Such hypotheses have been investigated using computer simulations and, recently, during Oceanic voyages in reconstructions ('floating hypotheses') of ancient voyaging canoes. Whether such simulations and 'replicas' can tell us anything about the original exploration and settlement of Remote Oceania depends on whether reliable data about the past is available, or valid assumptions made, concerning:

- the ancient environment;
- the navigational abilities of their crew;
- the performance of the boats thought to have been used.

There is general agreement that sea levels and coastlines, and the weather at sea, in the period 1500 BC to AD 1500 would have been similar to today's. Moreover, there is evidence in several regions of the world, that, from the mid second Millennium BC, groups of seamen had developed the ability to navigate out-of-sight of land using non-instrumental ('environmental') methods. The third requirement – the type of boat used on late second Millennium BC to the mid second Millennium AD exploratory and settlement voyages, and its sailing capabilities – would appear to be difficult to establish, not least because information about early Oceanic boats is rare: there have been only two finds of any importance and there are insufficient remains to reconstruct the original hulls (see p.133). The earliest written and illustrated descriptions are by European explorers of the mid eighteenth century AD; and small-scale models and other representations are similarly known only from this late period. The oldest surviving, full-size boat is now in the British Museum (1771: 5-31.1): this is a small, sewn-plank boat that formerly had a single outrigger. The third requirement, the capabilities of the exploration boats, is thus difficult, maybe impossible, to determine.

In 1975-1977, a double hulled (paired) boat, *Hokule'a*, and two single outrigger boats, *Taratai 1* and *2*, were built using twentieth century methods and tools. The hull shape of *Hokule'a* was based on eighteenth century descriptions of Tahitian/Tuamotan hulls. Her rig was derived from Hawaiian petroglyphs: crab-claw sails set on masts stepped on the centreline of the platform which joined together the two hulls. She measured 62 ft 4 in x 17 ft 6 in x 2 ft 6 in (draft) (19 x 5.33 x 0.76 m) and was manned by a twelve–man crew.

The aims of the several voyages undertaken by *Hokule'a* were to establish the sailing ability of Oceanic, paired boats and to investigate the feasibility of traditional navigational methods. It was established that *Hokule'a* could be sailed 70° off the wind (including 10° leeway) in calm to moderate, open-sea conditions, and 75° off the wind (15° leeway) in rough seas. The trials also confirmed Dr David Lewis' early-1960s conclusions that Oceanic navigational techniques were, indeed, reliable. It should be noted, nevertheless, that the results of such navigational investigations are only applicable to settlement voyages undertaken after distant islands had been discovered. It would be difficult, probably impossible, to re-enact an exploratory voyage during which nothing would be known of what lay ahead in terms of land, sea-state and weather. Dr David Lewis' opinion was that Oceanic craft were sailed 'full and by' (sails full and not lifting or shaking), as obtained in most sailing communities before early twentieth century, recreational sailors over-emphasised the requirement to sail as close as possible to the wind.

**NAVIGATION**
European seamen who 'discovered' the South Pacific islands needed compass, chart, logline, astronomical tables, telescopes and other aids to find their way within Oceania. There they encountered Oceanic seamen whose ancestors had settled widely-separated groups of

islands, within an enormous ocean. How had they done so, without instruments but using Stone Age technology?

Captain Cook answered that question: "— the Sun is their guide by day and the Stars by night, when these are obscured they have recourse to the points from whence the Wind and the waves of the Sea come upon the vessel". Joseph Banks, Cook's chief scientist, enlarged on this: "— of these (stars) they know a very large number by name, and the cleverest among them will tell in what part of the Heavens they are to be seen in any month when they are above the horizon. They know also the time of their annual appearance and disappearance to a nicety —. The people excel much in predicting the weather".

Andia y Varela, who led a Spanish expedition to Tahiti in 1772-6, noted that Oceanic sailing masters, known as *faatere*, divided the horizon into sixteen 'points' based on an E/W line between sunrise and sunset. They knew which stars rose and set on the bearings of all islands around them, and they gave each star the name of its associated island.

Unknown to these eighteenth and nineteenth century European seamen, these Oceanic, non-instrumental methods of navigation (Fig.7.10) were generally similar to those that had been used, in earlier days, in the Indian Ocean, the Mediterranean, and the European Atlantic. The principals of this 'environmental navigation' were evidently the same worldwide; their application varied, depending on latitude and weather pattern. The many islands of the South Pacific were mostly within 20° of the Equator where the night sky appears to rotate much less obliquely than in Atlantic Europe. Thus stars rose and set close to the vertical (as did the sun in daylight): this significantly extending their use as directional aids by day and by night. Mastery of such navigational aids enabled Oceanic seamen to explore the South Pacific Ocean in a deliberate manner, leading to settlement on just about every habitable island that existed.

Expanded targets
When exploring, Proto-Polynesians did not merely sail away with whatever wind was blowing in the hope that they would encounter

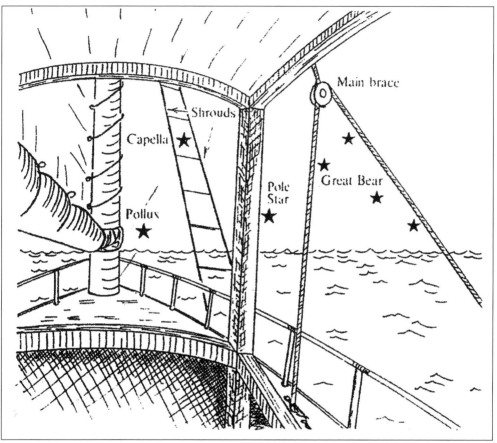

*7.10. Micronesian seamen steering by Polaris and Ursa Major. (after Lewis, 1994)*

land somewhere. They used environmental clues that indicated that there was land in particular sectors beyond the visible horizon. Such early warning of land can be given by:

- the flight line of sea birds that nest ashore;
- reflections of the predominant sea swell;
- certain cloud types form over islands; other types break-up;
- reflections from lagoons on atolls appear as a shimmering column in the sky;

- naturally occurring fires;
- the smell of land, land breezes and drifting timber.

Environmental navigation

The process of navigating without instruments is greater than the sum of its parts. Although aspects of it ('direction', speed' etc) have to be discussed (and may be analysed) separately, in practice the position of the boat is deduced from several, simultaneous observations, none of which are measured precisely. This environmental method of navigation is an art *par excellence:* past experience is used to examine the states of (mostly) independent variables – the relative positions of heavenly bodies; weather aspects; swell direction; movement of the boat through the water, the wake angle, and so on. The process is continuous, from taking departure from a known point of land to making a landfall in the vicinity of the intended destination.

Specialist techniques would have been required on exploratory voyages, searching uncharted seas for land beyond the horizon. On such voyages navigators would have had to maintain a 'mental plot' of the boat's position relative to the home base. If land was found it was also 'plotted'. When geographical closure was completed by successfully returning home, the original estimate of the outbound track would be amended. On subsequent passages to this 'new-found' land, on the other hand, track and distance (however they were measured) would both be known. Thus on such repeat passages, the boat's position would be 'plotted' as deviations from this standard track and distance.

Recent experimental voyages have been, in effect, repeat passages: although charts and other instruments may not be used, the participants know the track and distance from 'home' to destination. The conditions in which the earliest, exploratory voyages were undertaken cannot be replicated on a twenty-first century experimental voyage.

Taking departure

Before embarking, the South Pacific navigator would have checked the bearing of sunset and sunrise against landmarks, and the weather outlook ascertained. Before loosing sight of land he would 'take departure' by estimating his position relative to known landmarks: this would be the first datum on his 'mental chart'.

## Directions

Micronesian navigators who maintained some of their non-instrumental practices into recent times, used the swell/wind, the sun and notable stars as bases for their directional systems – key stars were those known to rise or set over each destination. A course was set and steered relative to whichever directional datum was dominant at a particular time – for example the celestial pole could be held on the port bow, the swell kept on the starboard quarter or the rising sun positioned fine on the starboard bow. Each system can be generalised to obtain what we would call a 'wind rose' or a 'star rose'. In Oceania, such 'roses' ('compasses') are concepts rather than instruments. Since these natural phenomena are not regularly spaced around the horizon, they cannot divide the horizon into equal sectors and so may appear unusual to twenty-first century European eyes.

## Distance, speed and time

David Lewis noted that Micronesian navigators appeared to judge speed by eye – possibly by the integrated assessment of spray, turbulence and wind pressure: it was probably described as 'usual' or 'less (or more) than usual'. As appears to have been common, worldwide, distance was understood as so many 'days' sail'. By day, the passage of time would be estimated from the sun's position relative to the 'fixed' times of sunrise, noon and sunset; by night by the sky's regular rate of rotation of 15° each hour.

## Keeping the reckoning

Recent Micronesian navigators on passage kept their reckoning using a process known as *etak*. This was a mental procedure by means of which information from several sources (wind, sea, sun, stars), estimates of speed and time, and summations of leeway and drift were integrated and then 'plotted' on the 'mental chart' to give the boat's position relative to a distant island (more or less on the beam). To the navigator, such islands apparently moved from 'one point of the compass' to another, on a reciprocal track to that of the boat that was considered to be stationary. As the voyage progressed, different reference islands were chosen. This *etak* seems to have been the key to successful navigation without instruments.

During the short, tropical twilight, towards the end of the day, most, if not all, sources of information could be used, leading to more reliable estimates of position. Dr David Lewis, an experienced Oceanic navigator, considered that a longer voyage did not mean greater inaccuracy: errors due to un-anticipated environmental changes, or to poor estimates of direction or speed, did not necessarily accumulate in one direction. Indeed, Lewis found that, over a long passage, they seemed to cancel out.

Landfall

'Dead on the nose' accuracy was not needed, not only because of the 'expanded target' phenomenon, but also because South Pacific islands were frequently found to be in groups: land could be sighted anywhere forward of the beam and, if it proved not to be the island intended, course could be altered for other, visible islands. Courses steered towards the end of a passage could be intentionally biased up-wind so that, at landfall, the boat would not be downwind of its destination. In a similar fashion, if there was a possibility of over-running a target during the night, the boat would be hove-to until daylight.

Navigation in Oceania

Dr. Lewis and other, more-recent, investigators have demonstrated that *etak* and its associated procedures provide a coherent system for navigating without instruments in tropical latitudes. The imprecision in the methods used are evidently offset by the *etak* evaluation of a range of data before a conclusion is reached, and by the cushioning effect of the extended range at which early warning can be obtained of land ahead. Would-be Oceanic navigators had to memorize a vast quantity of data and apply it to situations that never exactly repeated themselves: an Oceanic navigator was a true master of his profession.

The navigational methods described above are deduced to have been used in late-eighteenth century Micronesia: similar methods are likely to have been used in Polynesia. It is not possible to be certain, however, that they were used in the Oceanic migration period (1500 BC to AD 1000). Nevertheless, when differences in latitude and predominant weather are taken into account, it can be seen that the techniques used in eighteenth century Micronesia are generally similar to those used in the Classical Mediterranean and in early-medieval, Atlantic Europe. It thus seems likely that, at an early date, similar methods evolved, worldwide.

Implicit in these navigational methods is that the navigator knows his destination and is familiar (from personal or handed-on experience) with the route, with nearby, but invisible, lands on passage, and with the area around the destination island. Aspects of this navigational ability may also have been useful during exploratory passages, but it is difficult to see precisely how such techniques would have been applied during a first passage into unknown seas.

# CHAPTER 8

# The Americas

The American continent extends from *c.* 85° N. to *c.* 5° S, embracing all climatic zones (Fig.8.1). The northern parts of North America and the southern parts of South America extend well beyond the 40° N to 40° S zone in which rafts may be safely used at sea. America's western coasts face the Pacific Ocean, its eastern, the Atlantic, while to the north and south are the Arctic and Antarctic: thus American seafarers faced every type of maritime weather. Inland, the Americas include some of the finest river systems in the world.

## FIRST SETTLEMENT

Despite years of intensive and extensive research, the date of the first peopling of the Americas continues to be elusive: informed opinion is that it was probably before 15,000 BC, and may have been as early as 30,000 BC. It is generally agreed that the pioneering explorers came to Alaska from eastern Siberia (Fig.8.2). Whether they had to undertake a sea passage to reach Alaska depends on the precise date since, after 30,000 BC, sea levels worldwide generally rose, but with some transient reversals. The environmental evidence now available cannot be taken as definitive, but it suggests that overland travel from Siberia to Alaska would have been possible before 45,000 BC and also between 25,000 and 14,000 BC; whereas, seagoing water transport would have been needed between 45,000 and 25,000 BC, and after 14,000 BC. 'Overland travel' does not imply 'dryshod' since, in those times of lower sea level, the River Yukon would have meandered across 'Beringia' making it difficult terrain unless river transport were used.

*8.1. Map of the Americas.*

161

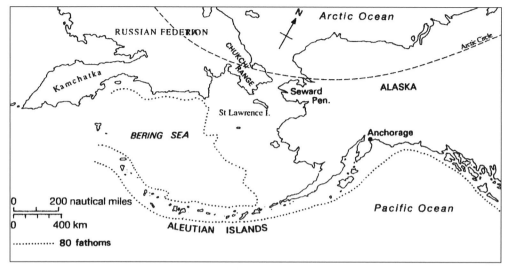

*8.2. Map of the Bering Sea region.*

Floats and rafts could not have been used at any time for a sea crossing along this route because of low sea and air temperatures, and the simple hide boats that could have been built in the Palaeolithic would not have protected the crew from cold winds and seas. With a Mesolithic technology, however, framed hide boats built from several hides, and therefore of some size, would probably have been sufficiently seaworthy and protective to be used to cross the Bering Strait, or to undertake a passage further south through the Aleutian Islands, from Kamchatka to the Alaskan peninsula.

It is now recognised that, in prehistoric times, a generally homogenous circumpolar culture became established from North Cape in Norway, eastwards across Eurasia to the Chukchi Sea in north-east Siberia, across to Alaska and northern Canada, and on to Greenland. This demonstrates that contacts could be established and maintained between Asia and America in those northern latitudes. Similarities in boat building techniques within this zone can be seen today: the Siberian hide boats, *baidara* and *baidarka* are similar to the Eskimo *umiak* and *kayak*; and the bark boats of the River Kutenai in British

162

Columbia are comparable with those of the River Amur in south-east Siberia.

At first sight, movement southwards from Alaska would seem to have been impossible until *c.* 16,000 BC as the way was blocked by the vast ice sheets of the Condillera, Laurentian and Greenland glaciers. It may, however, have been possible during the summer months to move southwards towards warmer latitude, on an inshore, coastal route protected by islands whenever possible, using the advanced form of hide boat that could be built in the Mesolithi*c*. Earlier, but with less certainty, such voyages may have been possible in the Palaeolithic, in simple hide boats.

## SUBSEQUENT SETTLEMENTS?

After the earliest movement of people from Asia eastwards into Alaska, there appear to have been three other periods when further settlements took place:

- two-way traffic between Alaska and Siberia across the Bering Strait, via the St Lawrence and the Diomedes islands;
- Scandinavian settlements from *c.* 900 to 1400 AD on the south and west coasts of Greenland;
- brief excursions by Scandinavians to Newfoundland around 1,000 AD.

The first of these appears to have been persistent but localised; the second and third were not only localised, but also transient. The main body of archaeological opinion is that the aboriginal population of America remained virtually free from external influences until 1492 AD. There is, however, other evidence to be considered of possible contact with America from Africa and from the South Pacifi*c*. Bottle gourds, considered to be native to Africa, have been excavated from some early South American sites: it is now thought likely that they had drifted there across the Atlanti*c*. The sweet potato, a native plant of America, was found on Oceanic islands by some of the earliest European explorers, leading to the suggestion that these had been

163

brought there on pre-Columbian voyages between Chile/Peru and Polynesia. Although anthropologists Hornell, Heyerdahl and others have argued for such early voyages, the simplest (and probably correct) explanation is that the earliest reports of Oceanic sweet potatoes are, in fact, late enough for the first plants to have been taken there by Spanish ships. On the other hand, there is general support for the suggestion that Oceanic seafarers, progressing eastwards in their colonisation of the South Pacific islands, may have made contact with the western coast of South America, but not until medieval or later times.

## WATER TRANSPORT

A number of logboats have been excavated in the Americas; there are also a number of early models and representations of rafts and possibly of other forms of water transport. These apart, the evidence for American water transport consists principally of descriptions and drawings compiled by eighteenth to nineteenth century Europeans. Many of these chroniclers, and some of the illustrators, were also seamen thus, after critical evaluation, the picture of early-American water transport that can be built-up from these accounts is likely to be reasonably accurate.

Discounting pottery boats (examples of which, worldwide, have only ever been noted in Egypt and China), there are (or have been) American examples of all the basic types of water transport: rafts of logs, bundles and floats; and boats of logs, bundles, bark, hides, baskets and planks. Specialised raw materials were required to build each type of water transport: for example, substantial logs for logboats and log rafts; tree bark with special properties for bark boats; particular oils and tars to make plank boats watertight. There has been a tendency, therefore, for each raft and boat type to have been devised and built in similar climatic zones in particular American geographical areas, one north and one south of the equator.

Log rafts

*Seagoing rafts.*

Early European explorers noted great seagoing rafts under sail between latitudes 30° N and 20° S, off Peru and California on the west coast, and in Brazilian waters off the east coast. Even at the relatively late date (1525) of the first of these observations, it is most unlikely that these rafts had been influenced by European technology. The west coast sailing rafts were built in a distinctive style: their lowest layer consisted of twenty or thirty logs, some 40 ft (12 m) in length, roped together; a second layer was spaced out across these primary logs and fastened to them by treenails; above this, a series of vertical posts supported a further one, or even two, 'decks' of logs so that the superstructure rose to about 10 ft (3 m) above the waterline.

Such rafts undertook west coast passages of 1,500 miles, from Lima to Panama. Europeans estimated that they could carry sixty to seventy tons of cargo: robust goods were carried at the lowest level; the crew, with their possessions, were in the 'room' at the middle level and vulnerable cargo was stowed on the 'deck(s)' above them. Typical of the loads carried are: thirty large casks (*toneles*); and fifty men and three horses.

On an early-seventeenth century drawing by George van Spilbergen of a sailing raft in Paita harbour (Fig.8.3), the crew are depicted adjusting devices now known by the Spanish term, *guares* – boards, 5–6 ft (2 m) in length, with an aerofoil cross section (see p.54, 94–6, 103, 109–111). The handle at the top of each *guares* was used to adjust its position between the logs of the raft. By varying position and depth of immersion, course could be altered, sailing balance adjusted and leeway reduced. For example, increasing the depth of immersion of a *guares* near the bow or moving it even closer to the bow, would cause the raft to turn towards the wind; raising or removing one near the stern would have a comparable effect. *Guares* projecting to varied depths may be seen on drawings of sailing rafts published by Admiral Pâris. Several of these 'variable leeboards' have been excavated from graves at Ica in Peru (Fig.8.4). The earliest of them is dated to *c.* 300 BC, thus this steering technique was pre-Columbian.

8.3. 17<sup>th</sup> century sailing log raft in Paita harbour, with guares in use: a detail from Spilbergen's drawing.(after de Bry)

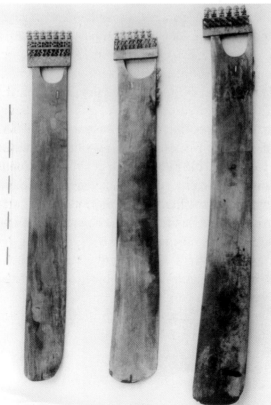

8.4. Variable leeboards (guares) excavated from c. 300 BC graves in Ica, Peru. (Paul Johnstone)

*Inshore and riverine rafts*
Inshore, and on inland waters, simpler forms of raft were used for fishing and the carriage of passengers and cargo. Belzoni, in the late sixteenth century, reported that Ecuadorian inshore rafts were shaped at the ends by using an odd number of logs with the longest one in the middle. A further refinement was achieved by orientating each log so that its butt end was at the stern: the natural taper of each log produced a hydrodynamically-advantageous, waterline shape, broader aft than forward.

Bundle rafts
Pizarro sighted reed bundle rafts fishing off the Peruvian coast, during his 1531 voyage. They were later noted off Chile and as far north as San Francisco in California. The distribution of such sea-going rafts subsequently proved to be between 40° N and 35° S. Others were seen on the rivers and lakes of west coast states and in Brazil and Argentina. Bundle rafts ranged in size from one-man 6 ft (1.8 m) caballito, used as ship's tenders, to the 15–20 ft (4.5–6 m) sailing rafts of Lake Titicaca which could carry twelve passengers and their baggage. Caballito built in Lima during the nineteenth century weighed only a few pounds so that a fisherman's mule could carry not only a raft, but also the man's net and material to build a hut.

Bundle rafts were made of reeds, rushes or palm. Rafts on the Lower Mississippi had two layers of cane bundles, the cane being carrizo which was found to be both buoyant and water-resistant. The simplest rafts consisted of two bundles lashed side-by-side: the paddler sat astride. Larger ones were 'boat-shaped' either pointed at both ends or with a blunt stern: these were used on inland waters whilst, in general, the seagoing ones were smaller. Rafts could be given extra 'freeboard' by adding smaller bundles to the upper outer sides. The essential steps when building such rafts were:

- reeds were specially selected and were harvested at a particular time of year;
- bundles were bound tightly to make the craft more rigid and less liable to waterlogging (Fig.8.5);

*8.5. Binding together a two-bundle reed raft in South America.*

- Lashings of cotton, rush vines *etc.* were used to join bundles together using coiled basketry techniques (linking together, and further binding-in, each bound bundle).

Additionally, Chumash Indians of the Californian coast coated their rafts of low-quality reed with a boiled mixture of locally-available bitumen and pine pitch. This waterproofed them and effectively turned them into bundle boats.

Buoyed rafts
Buoyed rafts used in two regions derived their buoyancy in different ways: in Mexico and northern Peru, from gourds held in a plant-fibre net; in southern Peru and northern Chile, from two inflated, multiple-hide floats (Fig.8.6). In both cases, crew, cargo and passengers used a

'deck' of light timbers. The rafts with netted gourds were used as river ferries, and were propelled by swimmers – one pulling, one pushing. It has been suggested that the hemi-spherical object depicted underneath rafts on a golden disc from Chichen Itza in Yucatan, were gourds. If so, this would take their earliest known use back to *c.* AD 500.

*8.6. A buoyed raft in Valparaiso, Chile. (Admiral Pâris)*

Coastal fishermen in Peru and Chile lashed together two inflated, multi-hide floats to form a seagoing raft. Such craft were elongated and were tied together tightly at the bow but further apart at the stern, thus producing a 'boat-shaped' raft. Each float was formed by sewing together several seal skins using fish-bone awls, wooden or bone toggles and lashings of seal intestines. The seams of these floats were sealed with grease and then payed with two or three coats of a mixture of red clay, grease and oil.

Seagoing float-rafts averaged *c.* 2–3 m in length and *c.* 1.25 m across the stern. They were occasionally propelled by a small cotton sail, but more usually by double-bladed paddles which were also used in *kayaks* and in sewn plank boats: such paddles seem to have been unique, worldwide. Buoyed rafts were used to transport people and goods across river estuaries, and also to and from ships anchored off-shore. Those sea passages were often through surf in conditions in which a European boat would have been swamped: the last recorded use in this role was in 1944.

### Bark boats
Bark boats were used in three separate regions: in a vast area of North

America (Fig.8.7), south of the hide boat zone (which extended as far south as 65°–60° N.); on the rivers of Guiana and Brazil, especially the Amazon; and on the west coast of southern Chile (Fig.8.8), south of the plank boat region. Europeans who first saw such canoes were impressed by their speed under paddles: Captain Weymouth, for example, noted that such a boat with a crew of three overtook his ship's boat propelled by four oarsmen. Bark boats were used by native Americans in coastal seas and in the deeper rivers, and were also extremely useful in rivers with rapids. The bark boat's light weight

*8.7. A canot de maître shooting rapids in the early-20th century.*

*8.8. Bark boats in Tierra del Fuego. (after Johnstone, 1988)*

meant that not only could it be readily carried overland, but also its buoyancy gave it good speed potential and an impressive cargo capacity. Europeans found them to be ideal for 'wilderness travel' since they could be repaired using materials to hand; indeed, a new boat could be built using resources available close to rivers. So impressed were the French with the bark boat that, by the mid eighteenth century, they had them built in a factory established near Montreal.

*Tools*

Special tools – knives, wedges, scrapers and wooden rollers- were used to harvest suitable bark sheets. Knives and awls were used to bind and sew the sheets; axes, knives and mallets to make, assemble and fasten the framing. A curved knife of distinctive shape was used by early-twentieth century bark boat builders to fashion the ribs – the possibility that this could be a diagnostic feature of earlier bark boat-building remains to be investigated.

*Building materials*

The northern bark boat region extended from Newfoundland and New England in the east, to Alaska and British Columbia in the west. This region more or less coincided with the range of the paper birch tree, the bark of which was considered to be the most suitable for boatbuilding since it was resinous and flexible and did not shrink or stretch unduly. Furthermore, this bark had a horizontal grain which facilitated sewing several sheets together, using as thread roots of black spruce, cedar, larch and pine split into four strands. Appropriate gores (v-shaped segments) were cut out of this extended sheet and sewn together to form the required hull shape. A framework of stringers, ribs and thwarts was then made from white cedar, spruce or maple, forced into the bark shell and lashed there.

*Boat shape*

Although the bark boats of each tribe or tribal grouping had distinctive hull details, the great majority of North American boats seem to have had a shape generally similar to that of one particular boat brought from New England to Chatham in S.E. England in 1749, and recorded there. This 'Chatham' boat was double-ended; its breadth was maintained over the working area of the boat with a marked decrease towards the ends, resulting in 'hollow' lines at bow and stern. In long section, the sheerline remained parallel to the bottom over the working area, with a slight rise to the rounded bow and stern. In transverse section the boat was rounded throughout. Overall shape ratios: $L/B = 6.4$; $L/D = 11.8$; $B/D = 1.8$. Such a vessel would have been capable of speedy passages in relatively calm waters.

*Seagoing bark boats.*
In Newfoundland, New England and the Chilean archipelago specialist seagoing boats were built. In Newfoundland, Beothuk boats were 20 ft (6 m) long and 4 ft (1.22 m) broad, a foot or so broader than river boats of a similar-length. Their lower, transverse section was V-shaped, and there was a stout, longitudinal timber low down that has been described as a 'keelson' although it was not associated with a mast. On seagoing voyages between islands in the Gulf of St Lawrence and on coastal passages of fifty or so miles, stone ballast was carried.

The Micmac Indians of the New Brunswick coast hunted whales and seals in bark boats, 18–24 ft (5.5–7.3 m) in length. In transverse section these boats had 'tumblehome': that is, their upper sides turned inwards thus making it easier to drag seals over the gunwale, though keeping out heavy seas. As this tumblehome would have made paddling difficult, paddlers were stationed towards the ends of the boat where tumblehome was less pronounced.

*South American Bark Boats*
Whereas the bark boats of Guinea and Brazil have a simple structure, other South American bark boats – of southern Chile and offshore islands – are more complex: they are found in a zone extending from Taitao peninsula (*c.* 40 S°) to Cape Horn (56° S). In 1553, the first Spaniards to visit this region noted the bark boats of the Alacaluf and Yahgansu: they measured 15–25 x 3–4 x 2–3 ft (4.6–7.6 x 0.9–1.2 x 0.61–0.9 m) and were built from three sheets of bark (for example, from the Southern Beech) that was less than one inch thick – one sheet for the bottom and one for each side. Using stone or bone tools, these segments were fashioned to the required shape and lashed together with hide thongs over a caulking of a straw-mud mixture.

A framework of fifteen or more curved branches was lashed into that bark shell. The poles that ran along the upper edges of this framing were fastened together at bow and stern to match the tapered ends given to the bottom bark sheet: the ends of the boat thus became pointed. These poles also acted as sheerline stringers over which the two side sheets of bark were turned inboard and were then fastened to them by spiral sewing (there are similarities here with *umiak* hide boats). The shell of this boat was then lined with strips of bark from sheer to sheer. Crossbeams that ran across the boat from side to side were used as thwarts by the nine or ten paddlers.

### Hide boats

Sixteenth to nineteenth century Europeans, expanding into sub-Arctic and Arctic America and into inland parts of South America, encountered a variety of hide boats, ranging from those made from a single hide to more complex boats suitable for seafaring. The archaeological evidence for the early use of hide boats in America is mostly indirect until AD 500. In this respect, the American evidence is similar to that for hide boats in North–west Europe where there is little substantial evidence until first century BC accounts by Roman authors. Moreover, as also paralleled in north-west Europe, accounts of the use of such boats in medieval and post-medieval times, and their continued use into the modern age, strongly suggest that such usage had been firmly established in the prehistoric period. Supporting evidence for such long usage comes from the fact that, in historical times, hide boats have been the only type of water transport used by indigenous folk, from Asian eastern Siberia to Greenland in the Atlantic. Moreover, hide boats minimise requirement for timber – always in short supply in the Arctic and sub-Arctic: in recent times, animal bones have sometimes been used. Hide boats are very much in concord with the ecology of this circumpolar zone where few trees exist, yet there is a good supply of hides from land and sea animals.

The earliest, but indirect, evidence for such boats comes from western Alaskan sites dated 3,000–2,000 BC. Worked points, similar to the ends of recent toggling harpoons, have been excavated from these sites, leading to the suggestion that, as in recent times, hunting kayaks may have been used there. Large whaling harpoons with whalebone, toggle-harpoon heads, and lance blades have been dated to the mid second Millennium BC; an inflation mouthpiece for a harpoon float has been excavated from Umnak island in the Aleutians;

and what may well be an *umiak* is engraved on an ivory bodkin from Cape Krusenstern in western Alaska.

By 1,000 BC Inuit had progressed eastwards as far as Greenland. Sites on St Lawrence Island in the Bering Strait, dated 300 BC–AD 400, and near-contemporary sites on the Chukchi peninsula of eastern Siberia, show that sea mammals were hunted, and by the late-centuries BC, whaling appears to have started in this region. Harpoon supports, bird darts and float plugs suggest the use of *kayaks*; whaling harpoons suggest *umiaks*. Ivory models, dated to the early centuries AD, of these two boat types, full-size paddles, pieces of boat framing, and whaling-size harpoons have also been excavated. Models of kayaks, dated to AD 500–900, have rounded bottoms and flared sides, while *umiak* models of a similar date have flat-bottoms, as do twenty-first century *umiaks*. The greater part of an 11 m *umiak* framework, dated by radiocarbon to the fourteenth/fifteenth century, was found on the strand at Herlufsholm, northern Greenland in 1949 (Fig.8.9).

*8.9. The framing of a 14th/15th century umiak found in Greenland in 1949.*

The late-nineteenth/early twentieth century Inuit had a similar life-style to those Arctic dwellers of the 'Thule' culture whom sixteenth century European explorers encountered. From the third Millennium BC through to recent times, there is archaeological and then, ethnographic, evidence for cultural continuity. As far as can now be documented, the two boat types – *umiak* and *kayak* – reached their optimum design by, or even before, the early first century AD. These boats appear to have retained their essential features to the present day because they match both the environment in which such boats are used, and the functions they are required to fulfil.

*Simple hide boats*
Boats made from a single hide were used on rivers and lakes in several American regions, including Columbia, Venezuela, Brazil, Bolivia, Paraguay, Patagonia and Argentina; and, further north, by the Plains Indians, and the Malecites and the Algonkin of the north-east Maritime Provinces. The *pelota*, a single hide boat, sometimes built without a framework, was first noted in the eighteenth century by the explorer Viedma in Patagonia where they were used as river ferries. In the early nineteenth century the Jesuit, Martin Dobrizhoffer, described how such frameless, single-hide boats were built. The feet and neck of a raw bull's hide were cut-off and the resulting square-shaped hide was placed on the ground, hairy side down. The four sides were bent so that they stood vertically, and the material at each corner was bound together with a thong, thereby retaining the square shape. A tow-line was then made fast to this boat through a hole in one side and a swimmer towed the loaded boat across the river with a passenger sitting upon his baggage. Dobrizhoffer noted that such boats retained their shape until, after a long period of continuous rain, the hide became soft and collapsed. This could be remedied by inserting a series of branches to form a simple framework.

Occasionally, a similar boat, but of rounded form, was built. In this case, the upper edge of the hide was laced by thongs to curved sticks, and further sticks were inserted to reinforce the bottom. Alternatively, sub-rectangular shaped boats were made by lacing a rawhide thong through a series of holes pierced through the edges of the hide. As this thong was tightened, the sides of the boat were drawn upwards.

The Plains Indians of North America built an equally simple hide boat, known to Europeans as the 'bull boat' (Fig.8.10). Such readily portable boats were widely used as swimmer-towed, river ferries; alternatively, they were propelled by a kneeling paddler. These boats were of circular form and were described as 'a large tub of a buffalo skin stretched on a frame of willow boughs'. Some bull boats survived into the twentieth century and details of their structure were noted. Once a suitable hide had been obtained, such a boat could be built in a few hours. They were built 'shell-first': a hide (sometimes two) was fashioned to the required shape and made watertight; a light framing (consisting of widely-spaced withies, bound together where they crossed, and turned upwards along their length) was then inserted into that hide 'shell'. The withy ends were then joined together by a circle of withies to form the rim of the boat. A second withy circle was added to shape the bottom of the sides. The upper edges of the hide were then turned in over the rim and lashed to the framework. In this way, a bowl, some 4–5 ft (1.2–1.5 m) in diameter, was formed with a flat bottom and near-vertical sides. After periods of use, such boats were regularly smoked and oiled to preserve the hide.

*8.10. A Bull Boat of North Dakota: diameter 5 ft; depth 22 in; dry weight 38 lbs.*

In early Spring, when boats were needed but bark was not yet available, Malecite and Algonkin Indians built equally-simple, hide boats, but in a different sequence: the skeleton-first sequence, as used for bark boats. A boat-shaped framework was built and then covered with hides.

*The Umiak/Baidara*

The Alaskan *umiak* and the Siberian *baidara* were, structurally, the same. These seagoing, open boats consisted of a light, resilient framework of fir (*Abies sp.*) or spruce (*Picea sp.*) driftwood, made watertight by a covering of a semi-independent, assemblage of two to five walrus or seal skins: they were thus built 'skeleton-first'. Currents flowing from the Pacific coast of Asia brought driftwood to the Arctic, and currents from northern Russia, flowing via the Arctic Sea and Greenland brought it to the north-east American coast. Timbers fashioned from this driftwood were made into a lightweight, widely-spaced framework by fastening them together using sinew or hide thong lashings: such a structure made the vessel resilient.

A multi-hide 'skin' was then fitted to the framework so that it covered the entire boat except for handles protruding at each end (Fig.8.11). This 'green', untreated hide cover had been sewn together by thongs, using 'hidden' stitches which did not penetrate the hide but remained within its thickness at the overlapping seams. The upper edge of the cover was turned inboard over the top stringers and lashed to a pair of lower stringers. Having only this one set of fastenings meant that the shock of the boat hitting an obstacle, such as ice, was absorbed, since the whole 'skin' moved around the framework. Once fastened in position, the hides were dressed with seal oil and caribou fat and the seams were payed with blubber to delay degradation and ensure water-tightness. Unlike tanning, this treatment did not change the hide structure; moreover, the boat remained watertight for no longer than seven days as the sea leached out preservatives.

The length of each *umiak* was determined by available timbers and James Hornell, a renowned boat ethnographer of the early twentieth century, estimated that, in his day, the average one measured about 30

*8.11. A paddled kayak and an oared umiak with the sun shining through its framework. (after Paul Johnstone, 1988)*

*8.12. The cockpit and bows of a Greenland kayak.*

x 5-6 ft (9.1 x 1.5-1.8m). In earlier centuries, *umiaks* of 60 ft (18.2 m) length had been reported, while the largest one recorded in the twentieth century measured 10.67 x 1.37 x 0.61 m (*c.*35 x 4 x 2 ft).

*Umiaks* were generally steered by an oar pivoted at the stern. They were propelled by paddles or by oars pivoted against bone tholes or in thong loops. Their lightweight structure meant that they floated relatively high in the water, thus they had much windage and, in a strong wind, could be difficult to steer. In 1576, the explorer, Martin Frobisher, noted a *umiak* under sail, the mast of which was stepped in a block on the keelson; there was no mast thwart, but the mast was supported by hide stays & shrouds. In an illustration published by Admiral Pâris in the early nineteenth century, a *umiak* with a female crew is depicted with a mast stepped well forward, on which a square sail had been set with sheets but no braces. Such a rig would have been limited to use in a following wind. The helms-woman is depicted using a large, freely-held paddle to steer. No oar pivots are shown and the other four women appear to be paddling, but are facing aft! In recent times, *umiaks* have been used to move cargo and passengers, a role in which they were very efficient: an empty boat could be carried by two men, yet that boat afloat could carry two tons of cargo. In earlier times smaller, handier boats used for whaling were fitted with inflated floats fastened to the top stringer to prevent capsize. Such boats were preferred to their own whaleboats by Yankee whaler men working in north-west Alaskan waters.

### The kayak / baidarka

The *baidarka* of Siberia is generally similar to the Alaskan *kayak*. Like the *umiak*, the *kayak* combines strength with light weight, and its elongated, lanceolate form gives it the speed needed in its hunting role (Figs.8.11 & 8.12). The narrow beam and low freeboard, however, reduce its natural stability to the very minimum. This disadvantage is offset to a degree, and seaworthiness maintained, by having a watertight deck with the paddler's waterproof coat fastened to his cockpit coaming.

One obvious difference within this *kayak/baidarka* family is that, although most kayaks have only one cockpit, some Alaskan boats have two, or even three: in this they are similar to some eastern Siberian boats. It seems clear, however, that every Siberian and Alaskan kayak has a set of core attributes: this suggests that they are all variants of one particular boat type.

Like the *umiak*, *kayaks* are, and were, built in the skeleton sequence i.e. a framework was built and a 'skin' of hides added to it, the hull being pierced only by a cockpit (or cockpits) for the crew. In transverse section, the *kayak* hull was 'multi-chine', since the 'skin' closely conformed to the shape outlined by the framework of stringers. Longitudinally, the boat was very low, with a slight rise at the stern and a more pronounced one at the bow. Recent *kayak* users have emphasised how they have most confidence when man and boat feel and act as one.

*Kayaks* were built from the same raw materials as *umiaks*, except that willow (Salix sp.) was needed for the bent frames. This framework was lashed together, the top stringer being the primary strength member. Two to five hides were then joined together and stretched over this framework to form the *kayak's* 'skin'.

*Size and shape.* Nowadays, *kayaks* built for travelling are bigger than those built for hunting, and some have an enlarged cockpit, or two separate cockpits, to take two people back-to-back. In quiet waters, further passengers may travel spread-eagled on top of such boats. The smallest *kayak* ever known measured 4 x 0.50 x 0.24 m (13 x 1.6x 0.8 ft); the largest was 10 x 0.80 x 0.50 m (32 x 2.6 x 1.6 ft). The L/B ratio for a large group of hunting *kayaks* ranged from 15 to 9.5, and their L/D from 10 to 40. These figures highlight the fact that *kayaks* are long, narrow and low boats. They are also light weight, weighing only 25 to50 lbs (11–23 kg). This makes them good load-carriers: a one-man *kayak* can carry 3.5 times its own weight, whereas, the *faering*, a four-oared, Viking Age planked boat had a multiple of 1.5.

*Handling characteristics.* A double-bladed paddle is used to propel and to steer a *kayak*. Some early reports suggested that a hunting *kayak* could carry sail, but this 'sail' was probably a screen rigged to hide the paddler's silhouette as he approached his prey. It has occasionally been reported that, on rivers, two, or even three, *kayaks* were lashed together, side-by-side: with the transverse stability thus increased, a makeshift sail could be rigged. Underway, the paddler automatically adjusts his body to maintain the boat in a stable state: when at rest, the paddler places one blade on the water surface. Because of the kayak's inherently low transverse stability, a special method of manning a boat has to be used. For similar reasons, a routine has been established to enable the paddler to recover after capsizing (a not infrequent occurrence): the paddler stays in his cockpit and uses his paddle to roll the boat upright again.

*Performance.* It has been estimated that, on passage in fair weather, the hunting kayak's maximum speed is around 5 knots. The boat's low profile and excellent manoeuvrability were great assets when hunting: stealth rather than speed was needed to stalk seals, walruses or whales at sea, or migrating caribou at river crossings.

Logboats
*Logboats on lakes and rivers*
Excavations on two islands off the eastern coast of Yucatan revealed fifth to ninth century goods, such as obsidian, metalwork and pottery, that had been carried by sea along a trade route that extended from the Aztec Mexican entrepôt at Xicalango in the Bay of Campach, around the Yucatan peninsula to the River Ulua in Honduras. Further north, a model logboat of jade has been found in Vera Cruz, Mexico. Documentary sources show that Aztecs used boats, especially in and around their capital, now Mexico City, where stone carvings on a temple depict 'punt-ended' logboats.

Seventeenth century European explorers also reported logboats on inland waters in Ecuador, North Carolina, Virginia, the north and east coast of South America, and on the great rivers, Mississippi, Orinoco,

Amazon and de la Plata. They have been excavated (few of them archaeologically) from sites stretching from Ontario and Quebec to Florida and Texas: most of these appear to have been fashioned from cypress (*Cupressus spp.*) or pine (*Pinus sp.*) logs. The oldest among those so far dated is one from Florida of 5120 BC; the most recent is from an Indian reservation in Ontario and is dated *c.* AD 1500.

In sum, logboats have been used on American rivers and lakes in three zones: North America – in the east, from the Great Lakes to the Mississippi and Florida; Central America – within the Gulf of Mexico and the Caribbean Sea; South America – in the northern and eastern regions. They were also used on the west coast (Fig.8.13), in Chile and Peru, although it may be that these were not indigenous but had been introduced by Europeans.

Sixteenth century accounts described two types of logboat on the Mississippi. The smaller ones (large, by European standards) were

*8.13. Mid-19$^{th}$ century logboats in Valparaizo, Chile. The one to the right and the one end-on have stabilising timbers fastened at their waterline and side-heightening washstrakes. (Admiral Pâris)*

around 10 m in length and 1 m in breadth: they had twenty-eight paddlers, stationed two abreast. The larger ones (up to 25 m in length) were used on warring raids, and held fifty paddlers and twenty-five to thirty warriors. Paddlers kept time by chanting, and achieved speeds of 8 to 12 knots.

*Seagoing logboats*
On his first trans-Atlantic voyage, Columbus came upon Caribbean logboats of great size: one was said to be as long as a 'galley of 15 benches' i.e. *c.* 50 ft (15 m). Such a boat made from a single log probably had a minimum breadth of at least 4 ft (1.22 m) and a breadth at the stern of *c.* 6 ft (1.8 m). On his second voyage, Columbus recorded an even larger boat some 96 ft (29 m) long and 8 ft (2.5 m) in breadth. These boats were more than twice the length and breadth of the largest, known European logboats. The European boats were for river and lake: the American boats, on the other hand, were sufficiently broad at the waterline to give them the transverse stability required to undertake inter-island passages – indeed, Columbus found them to be so used. Subsequent accounts describe large, Caribbean logboats that had been fitted with washstrakes – such boats would have had not only the stability, but also the freeboard, needed on seagoing voyages.

As Europeans ventured further along the American east coast, logboats of various sizes were noted throughout the Caribbean Sea and the Gulf of Mexico, off the coasts of Florida, Mexico, Honduras, Panama and Columbia. The largest of these would have had sufficient waterline breadth to carry sail safely: several were so noted, but details of their rig and their sailing abilities were not recorded.

Logboats were later encountered at sea on America's west coast, off British Columbia and Washington State, a region that included the Rivers Fraser and Columbia, and an archipelago of islands in the Strait of Georgia and Puget Sound. Excavations in the lower reaches of the River Fraser, and near a confluence in the River Columbia, have revealed that these were important salmon-catching areas from as early as the eighth millennium BC. The inhabitants of that region – Haida, Nootka, Wishram and Tlingit Indians – lived on an abundance of marine resources: whales, seals, sea lions, sea otters, seabirds, salmon, halibut and cod.

In the mid sixteenth century, Thomas Harriot described how he had seen logboats built in Virginia. The selected tree was felled by slowly burning through its bole, just above the roots. After the crown was similarly burnt off, the log was man-handled onto stocks so that its bark could be removed. The log was then hollowed by alternately slow-burning and then scraping with a shell that had been sharpened on sandstone.

In later centuries, European seaman, such as Captain Thomas Cook, recorded details of the seagoing logboats that they encountered. West Coast logboats, 9–11 m (30–35 ft) in length, destined to be used for hunting and fishing, were fashioned from a Red Cedar (*Cedrela odorata*) bole with a minimum diameter of 2 m. Such logs were hollowed using stone tools and fire to produce a boat with a flattish bottom and flared sides.

As has happened worldwide, the large logs needed for seagoing logboats eventually became unobtainable, and Americans turned to another technique: smaller logs were expanded to give a greater, waterline breadth. Water poured into a hollowed log was heated by hot stones until the timber became malleable. The sides were than slowly forced apart and framing timbers inserted so that, as the boat cooled, the expanded shape would be retained. The stage of forcing the sides apart to gain the final few degrees was always the most critical: it has been noted that, in Guyana, one in every four logs burst during this phase. After a successful expansion, not only had the waterline beam been increased, but also the ends of the boat had been forced to rise and the midships height of sides reduced: the result was that the expanded boat had a sheerline that rose from the midships station towards both ends. If that lower side height near amidships proved to be inadequate, washstrakes were added. This expansion technique has been used worldwide, wherever suitably malleable tree species existed; in the Americas, it has been used in recent times in Guyana, Brazil, Tierra del Fuego and Alaska. The process is well worth the effort, since a beamier, therefore more stable, boat is obtained.

An alternative way of increasing the stability of smaller logboats, and thus improving seagoing performance, was recorded in Valparaiso, Chile, by the mid nineteenth century Admiral Pâris; similar observations were made in Charca, Columbia, and, off the island of Gorgona by the early-twentieth century ethnographer, James Hornell. Logboats with an inadequate waterline breadth had a balsa log lashed to each side so that they floated alongside at the boat's waterline. These two 'stabilisers' effectively increased the boats' waterline beam, thus giving them the stability needed for seagoing.

Sewn-plank boats
Planked boats were found in use in only two widely-separated regions in the Americas, both on the west coast, in California and in Chile.

*North America – the Chumash tomol* (Fig.8.14)
These boats were used in the Santa Barbara channel, north of Los Angeles, from Point Conception at 34° 50′ N, south-eastwards to Point Mugu (34° N). The Chumash Indians had settled on a narrow strip of coastal land, cut-off to the east by a mountainous hinterland, and protected to the west by a belt of islands. The topography of this region, the bitumen that was readily available from surface springs, and a supply of cedar and pine driftwood, facilitated (perhaps, even stimulated) the building of plank boats, and may also have ensured that, subsequently, this specialised type of boatbuilding did not spread beyond this zone.

The *tomol* was first documented in the late eighteenth century, by which time the Chumash had been subject to European influences for more than 200 years and had been rapidly hispanicized. Nevertheless, the account of the building of a *tomol* compiled by Father Pedro Font in 1776 shows that they had adopted few, if any, European boatbuilding techniques – for example, they were using no tools other than shells and flints. The *tomol* described by Father Font was built of twenty or so long, narrow planks, joined together at the seams by lashings of deer-sinew, and waterproofed with bitumen: the outcome was a hull with a sheerline that rose towards the pointed bow and stern.

*8.14. A reconstruction of a tomol: the lashed plank boat of the Chumash Indians of the Santa Barbara Channel, north of Los Angeles. (Museum of Natural History, Santa Barbara)*

These boats had no ribs, merely one transverse timber near amidships that preserved the boat's shape and served as a thwart.

One such *tomol* is said to have measured '36 palms long and somewhat more than three palms high'. If this 'palm' is taken to be *c.* 4 inches, this boat was around 12 ft in length and 1 ft in height (of sides amidships?). Other *tomols* measured 5.2–6.7 m in length and 0.91–1.20 m in breadth; and 12–18 ft in length with 4 ft breadth amidships (3.7–5.5 m x 1.2 m). These reported dimensions give a ratio of L/B varying from *c.* 3.5 to 5.5.

The tools used to build early-twentieth century *tomols* included adzes, chisels and scrapers made from clam shells; augers of sharpened bone or flint; and sharkskin used as 'sandpaper'. At that time, the method of fastening the planking together and making it watertight, was described: a hot mixture (known as *yop*) of bitumen (*wogo*) and pine pitch, was placed along the plank edges and the two planks placed edge-to-edge; they were then lashed together with a waxed 'string' of red milkweed fibres (*tok*) – such fastenings were individual lashings rather than continuous sewing. Finally, each seam was caulked with *yop*.

In recent times the *tomol* was used for communication between mainland and islands, and for fishing those waters and in the open sea. *Tomol* boats were so light that they could be launched by two men. Loaded with fish, they could be carried on the shoulders of ten or twelve men. At sea, fishing boats were propelled by two paddlers, one near each end of the boat, with a boy stationed near amidships to bail out water. Double-bladed paddles were used, and, so that a steady course would be maintained, paddlers synchronised their stroke and simultaneously plied opposite blades. Other *tomols* carried passengers: in 1602, Sebastian Vizcaino noted that such a boat held fourteen or fifteen men, including eight paddlers.

Tomol boats fell out-of-use in the late nineteenth century before they had been fully documented: our knowledge is thus incomplete. Although attempts were made in the twentieth century to recover information by interviewing elderly Chumash, seeking out old boats, and building two 'reconstructions'(Fig.8.14), it must be said that only a partial understanding of this building tradition has been obtained. It is clear, however, that, in its prime, this, almost-unique, lashed-plank, seagoing boat was in tune both with its environment and with the uses it was put to by the coastal Chumach.

### South America – the Chilean dalca

The *dalca* was first noted in the mid sixteenth century during de Ulloa's expedition along the Chilean coast. They were subsequently found along the coast and among off-shore islands from *c.* 47° S, near the Gulf of Penas, through the Chonos archipelago to *c.* 42° 30′ S, in the Gulf of Coranados, north of the island of Chiloé. As with the Chumash *tomol,* the Chilean *dalca* was restricted to a region within a protective archipelago of numerous, off-shore islands.

Early accounts indicate that these 'double-ended', sewn-plank boats were originally built from three planks of larch, (*Fitzroya patigonica*), cypress (*Libocedrus tetragonal*) or beech (*Nothofagus betuloides*). A long, thick bottom plank curved upwards towards the ends, sometimes beyond the sheerline; and the two side planks converged towards the ends where they were fastened to the extended bottom plank. Planks were butted, edge-to-edge and the seams were caulked with either the inner bark of the *maqui* tree (*Aristolelia maqui*), or of *tiaca* leaves (*Caldeluvia paniculata*), or rolls of grass, or a mixture of herbs and clay. This caulking was held in place by a split-cane batten, and the planking was then fastened together over this batten by continuous sewing with a bamboo 'thread' (*Chusquea coley*). A series of transverse, round-wood timbers supported this plank shell and were also used as thwarts.

Planks were split from the log by wooden wedges, and stone or shell tools were used to build the *dalca*. Mid sixteenth-century *dalca* were 30–40 ft (9–12 m) in length and 3 ft (0.9 m) broad, and were propelled by single-bladed paddles, and could carry, it has been estimated, nine to eleven men. The lowest stitching in a *dalca* was above the bottom of the boat and thus was not damaged when the boat took the ground: indeed, they are known to have been dragged overland for a considerable distance without damage to their fastenings.

By the late eighteenth century several European features had been incorporated in the *dalca*, and five-plank and then seven-plank versions were built, nevertheless, they continued to have sewn fastenings. Under European influence, the use of this modified *dalca* spread southwards: the very last one was seen afloat in the Magellan Strait in 1915. Compared with the *tomol*, the *dalca* was technologically advanced since its planking was fastened by continuous sewing rather than lashings.

## AMERICA'S EARLIEST WATER TRANSPORT?

The Americas extend from *c.* 85° N to *c.*55° S and, as early Americans moved southwards from Alaska, they encountered different environments and a changing range of raw materials. This led to the building of similar types of water transport in widely separated locations, one north, and one south of the equator (Table 8.1).

## Table 8.1. Types of water transport built in North and South America

| | |
|---|---|
| Hide boats | North: from 85° N to 30°–40° N |
| | South: from 35° S to10° S |
| Bark boats | North: from 60° N to 45°- 35° N |
| | South: from 55° S to 25° S |
| Log boats | from 50° N to 30° S |
| Rafts | from 40° N to 40° S |
| Plank boats | North: at 35° N |
| | South: at 45° S |

**Notes**

1 Latitudes are approximations;
2. Rafts were used mainly on the west coast, but also in Brazilian waters and possibly in the Caribbean.

The data in Table 8.1 is based on 'first European contact' reports and is intended to reflect the pre-Columbian situation. Early reports on American water transport (from the late fifteenth century until the early seventeenth century) may be taken as reliable observations, both in general and in detail, especially those made by seamen, as many of them were. However, 'first contact' accounts continued to be compiled into the mid nineteenth century, by which time, European technological influences had spread widely. For this and other reasons, the distribution of logboats, given above, may not be as accurate as that of bark and hide boats. Despite such misgivings, there is reasonable evidence that there were two distinct groups of logboats: those on the west coast of North America, from Alaska to California (amongst which were great, seagoing vessels); and those of the east and south, from the eastern Great Lakes to Florida and Louisiana, the coasts and islands of the Gulf of Mexico and in the Caribbean, the north-east coast of South America and the basins of the East Coast rivers, Amazon and del Plata, and in Columbia and Ecuador on the West Coast.

Table 8.1 is a generalisation and uses generic names for groups that, in fact, include individual types of boat that differ significantly, one from another. Thus, the bark boats of southern Chile and the Amazon basin, although having a basic structure similar to that of the North American boats, were clearly inferior in performance to the more specialised northern boats. Similarly, the hide boats of the Plains Indians and those of inland South America were not only much less developed structurally but also of inferior performance when compared with the hide boats of America's Arctic region. In fact, when assessed by their effectiveness in a hostile environment, the seagoing, hide boats of North America appear to be among the very best in the world. Perhaps the only vessels of comparable excellence are the recent hide boats of Arctic Siberia (culturally related) and the seagoing, hide boats of early north-west Europe.

From the end of the fifteenth century onwards, as 'first contact' Europeans spread through the Americas, a wide range of water transport was observed both at sea and on lakes and rivers. Nevertheless, native ocean-going ships, comparable in size with those in Columbus' fleet, were never encountered. American vessels did undertake lengthy, sea passages but it was not 'noble ships' that Europeans observed off the coasts of California, Peru and Brazil, 'merely' log rafts. Notwithstanding the differences in potential, these seagoing rafts were of great size and capable of lengthy sea passages: loaded with tradable goods, for example, they are known to have been sailed on west coast passages from Lima to Panama, a distance of some 1,500 miles.

When humans first moved from Siberia into the Americas, they found no dramatic changes in the environment or in the raw materials available. Subsequently, on the migration southwards and eastwards from Alaska, as different environments were encountered, a range of water transport was developed which parallels achievements elsewhere in the world. It is possible that there was a two-way flow of ideas via *Beringia,* and/or across the Bering Strait, but this would have been limited to improvements to, and embellishments of, the hide boat. The other types of water transport that are deduced to have been within the Americas at first European contact, were almost certainly developed independently – sometimes more than once – as new environment were encountered and different raw materials became available, and as and when human ingenuity and technological competence determined.

## AMERICAN ACHIEVMENTS

Within the Americas, certain types of water transport, all of them seagoing craft, were developed that rivalled any from elsewhere in the world: Arctic hide boats; the logboats of the north west and of the Caribbean; bark boats of North America; bundle rafts of the Pacific coast, and the log rafts of South America with their *guares*.

Apart from hide boats, the specific versions of all the forms of American water transport observed at first European contact must have been invented within the Americas. Furthermore, some of the features and fittings found in these rafts and boats – for example, the double-bladed paddles of the *kayak*, the *tomol* and the buoyed raft – were unknown elsewhere. Moreover, the sail was independently invented there: sail shapes and rigging that were seen there by early Europeans have not been noted elsewhere.

A major feature, unexpected by Europeans, is the relative insignificance of the planked boat in pre-Columbian America. There were only two minor groups of sewn plank boat, in widely separated places on the coasts of southern Chile and California: the *dalca* with sewn planks, and the *tomol* with lashed. Only in those two places did special circumstances lead to the invention of the plank boat. Moreover, it was those circumstances – the local resources and the closed nature of those communities due to topography – that appear to have restricted those lashed- and sewn-plank techniques to these two zones.

An intriguing question arises if one supposes that European ships had not arrived in the Americas in the fifteenth century. If, as elsewhere, American economic, political and social life had developed to a position where large, seagoing vessels were required, could their seagoing log rafts and logboats have been developed to undertake oceanic voyages rather than coastal passages? Throughout the rest of the world, it was the boat built of wooden planks that had been developed into the ocean-going ship. Would those isolated coastlands of southern Chile and of California have become centres of innovation? Or were they so marginal and self-sufficient, and with a sustainable, symbiotic relationship to their environment, that the necessity for a larger and more seaworthy *dalca* or a *tomol* would never have arisen?

# CHAPTER 9

# In Conclusion

T
he picture of the early water transport of the world beyond Europe, presented in this volume, is incomplete. The relative size of each chapter is not a measure of the importance of that region's water transport in earlier times, rather, chapter length has depended on the quantity and quality of research undertaken and published by archaeologists, historians and ethnographers. Moreover, every chapter is biased by the limited range of raft and boat types excavated. Throughout the world, plank boats and (in certain regions) logboats, recorded archaeologically, significantly outnumber (sometimes exclude) all other forms of water transport: there is a corresponding bias in this volume. This disparity is, at least, partly due to the near-ephemeral nature of floats and rafts, and the fact that, when they are no longer sea-worthy, their constituent parts can readily be re-used. Boats mainly built of materials other than wood (for example, hide boats and bundle boats) also rapidly degrade when abandoned, increasing the bias in the sample of water transport that survives.

## EARLY WATER TRANSPORT

A more fundamental bias is that no excavated raft or boat remains are dated earlier than *c.* 7,000 BC, when there is evidence that water transport was used in much earlier times. Two examples may be given: around 40,000 BC (maybe earlier), humans passed through the Wallacean archipelago of islands on their overseas migration from Greater South–East Asia to Greater Australia; in *c.* 20,000 BC (possibly earlier) the Americas began to be populated either overland, during a period of low sea levels, or by water transport when (as now) there was sea between Siberia (in Euro-Asia) and Alaska (in the Americas).

194

IN CONCLUSION

Excavated examples of the several types of the world's water transport are relatively few in number: a handful (four?) of early rafts, and an increasing, yet still small, number of early bundle-boats (half-a-dozen?), logboats (a few hundreds?), and plank boats (perhaps one hundred, well-documented and dating earlier than AD 1500). There are no excavated examples of the four basic types of float; only one type (log) is known of the four types of raft, and a mere three types (log, plank & bundle), of the six forms of boat, have been excavated. Although, to a degree, the documentation of ethnographic examples of water transport fills those gaps, much archaeological fieldwork and targeted excavation remain to be undertaken.

**BUILDING TRADITIONS**
The identification of regional types of raft has not yet been attempted, nor have regional differences in boats other than planked ones been investigated. The regions discussed in this volume have developed their own plank boat types differentiated, one from another, by distinctive features. By medieval times, however, there were two building traditions – those of South-East Asia and China – that seem to have shared structural features. It may be that these overseas trading partners borrowed shipbuilding techniques from one another; or it may be that borrowing was one-way: future wreck excavations may clarify this matter.

Sewn-plank boats (excavated and ethnographic) have been noted in every region of the world except Australia where planked boats were evidently never built, although some mainland Australians did build bark boats with sewn fastenings. Characteristic differences between the sewn-plank boats of different regions have proved difficult to define. At present, there appears to be one distinguishing feature: plank fastening are either individual lashings or continuous sewing. Rather than this being a regionally distinctive trait, however, this difference is probably temporal: lashings, early; sewing, later.

**THE RANGE OF BOAT TYPES**
As sea levels rose, early Tasmanians and subsequently, early

195

Australians, were cut-off from external influences at a time when they appear not to have progressed technologically beyond the Palaeolithic stage of building simple log rafts, bundle rafts, and (in Australia only) bark boats (some lashed, others sewn). Otherwise, in every region of the world so far studied, a wide range of water transport was conceived, built and used, mainly limited by the range of raw materials available.

Technologically, the plank boat was the most advanced form of water transport; moreover, it was the only type of water transport that could be developed into a ship. It is remarkable, therefore, to find that, in the Americas, the plank boat was used in only two small areas of the west coast (Fig.8.1): in South America, between the Gulf of Penas and the island of Chiloé; in North America, in the Santa Barbara Channel, north of Los Angeles. Moreover, the planking of the North American *tomol* was not sewn together but lashed, an elementary (and probably early) form of plank fastening. This relative insignificance of the plank boat in the Americas is remarkable in a land where the bark canoe and the hide boat reached a higher technological standard than probably anywhere in the world; where coastal passages were undertaken in sailing log rafts and in sailing logboats built from enormous trees; where distinctive types of sailing rig had been evolved and a unique form of buoyed raft developed; and where the double-bladed paddle seems to have been invented.

**FUTURE RESEARCH**

Identifying a wreck's 'home port'

Rafts, boats and ships travel and may be wrecked (hence enter the archaeological record) far from their place of origin: this mobility may easily be overlooked. Several near-contemporary, medieval wrecks, some excavated from the sea off South-East Asia and others off the Chinese coast, have structural features in common: built frame-first with bulkheads and multi-layer planking (Ch. 5 & 6). As there was overseas trade between those regions, Chinese ships may have been wrecked off South-East Asia, and South-East Asian ships wrecked in Chinese waters. The origin of each wreck has therefore to be determined by criteria other than the position of the wreck site. In future, the identification of the species of timber used and the acquisition of dendro-chronological data from those timbers should lead to the recognition of a ship's origins.

## *Guares*

Adjustable, foil-shaped, lee boards (*guares*) were used from at least 300 BC, in tropical/sub-tropical waters off the American west coast (Ch.8). In recent centuries they have been noted in use in the coastal waters and rivers of China, South-East Asia and India (see p.54, 94–6, 103, 109–110, 165–66). These *guares* were mainly used to steer sailing log-rafts and to achieve sail balance. Some authors have suggested that this trait may have been transferred from region to region by sixteenth century European ships on passage from the Atlantic through the Pacific to the India Ocean. An alternative explanation could be that, centuries earlier, *guares* were invented independently in each of those four regions; or (more likely?) it may be that they were invented in one of those regions and their use spread to other oceans by seagoing, sailing log rafts. Further research is also needed here.

## The Earliest Use of Sails

At present, the earliest evidence for sail, worldwide, is an image of a vessel with a bipod mast on a ceramic disc dated sixth to fifth millennium BC, from As–Sabiyah in Kuwait (see p.26) The earliest dates for the appearance of sail around the world (mostly from representational evidence) seem to show that, from the Persian Gulf – Egypt region, sail spread:

- westwards and northwards to the Mediterranean (2000 BC), to north-west Europe (500 BC) and on to the Baltic (seventh century AD); and,
- eastwards to India (2000 BC) and on to China (by 1200 BC?).

There must, however, have been at least one other place of origin: the sail must also have been independently devised in the Americas, since sixteenth and seventeenth century European seamen reported a unique range of sail types and rigs on both east and west American coasts.

Early sea passages

The use of sail introduced a step-change in the potential of water transport, wherever it occurred. Since, on present evidence, that date is relatively late (after *c.* 6,000 BC), sail cannot have been used on the earliest-known sea passages of 40,000 BC. Those early passages were undertaken in the warmer seas of the world between 40°N and 40°S, within sight of land, using log, or inflated-hide floats ancillary to swimming, or possibly onboard paddled rafts of logs or of hide-floats. Outside these latitudes (for example, on the north-west coast of America, at a later date), it may have been possible to use the simple hide boat in the summer months.

Visual pilotage techniques would have been used to keep the reckoning on those early passages. On present evidence, it seems likely that out-of-sight-of-land, navigational techniques were perfected in the early to mid second Millennium BC: from that time open-sea passages would have been possible. These theoretical ideas need to be confirmed or rejected by further research.

Experimental Archaeology

When compared with the amount of publicity given to Experimental Boat Archaeology during the past thirty years, such experimental work has contributed relatively little to our knowledge of former times. In the main, this has been because most of those projects were undertaken in a less-than-scientific manner: conclusions drawn were not securely based on demonstrable evidence. Moreover, in almost every such project, the focus of effort has been on the building and (especially) the trials of such vessels rather than on the hypothetical transformation of the excavated remains – incomplete, disturbed and fragmented – into a scale-model of the original vessel's form, structure, propulsion and steering. Future experimenters must understand that, only if such a model successfully undergoes informed criticism, should the building of a full-scale reconstruction be attempted.

# IN CONCLUSION

To date, experiments judged valid on those criteria are pitifully few: possibly only the Danish experiment to reconstruct, build and sail the five Viking Age, Skuldelev wrecks excavated from Roskilde fjord; and the Anglo-American-Greek project to design, build and use a 'floating hypothesis' of a fifth century BC Athenian trireme. These two experiments seem to have produced reconstructions that were as close as it is now possible to get to the original prototypes.

## Ethnographic research

In early twentieth century Oceania, boats were built with bone and stone tools. The Nootka Indians of North America's west coast used bird bones to bore holes in timber, and the Chumash Indians of California used flints and whalebone wedges to build seagoing, sewn-plank boats. In other parts of the world, shells were used for tasks that, today, we would use axe, adze or scraper: such a simple, non-metal tool kit could be used to build splendid examples of the boatbuilder's art. Further boat ethnographic fieldwork, in parts of the world that are not yet 'developed', should help increase our understanding of the way early boatbuilders pursued their calling.

# Further Reading

**General**

Anderson. A. Barrett, J.H. & Boyle, K.V. (ed) 2010. *Global Origins & Development of Seafaring*. Cambridge: McDonald Institute Monographs.

Anon. 2001. *Dictionary of the World's Watercraft*. Mariners' Museum: Newport News. and London: Chatham Publishing

Delgado, J. (ed).1997. *Encyclopaedia of Underwater & Maritime Archaeology*. London: British Museum Press.

Greenhill, B. 1995. *Archaeology of Boats and Ships*. Conway Maritime Press.

Hornell, J. 1946. *Water Transport.* Cambridge: Cambridge University Press. repr. 1970, Newton Abbot: David & Charles.

McGrail, S. 2004. *Boats of the World*. 2nd (paperback) edition. Oxford : Oxford University Press.

McGrail, S. 2014. *Early Ships and Seafaring: European water transport.* Barnsley: Pen & Sword.

*International Journal of Nautical Archaeology.* Journal of the Nautical ArchaeologySociety: Fort Cumberland. Portsmouth. PO4 9LD.

**Note:** Greek and Roman authors, writing between 700 BC and AD 100, illuminate aspects of the early maritime world: Homer; Herodotus; Julius Caesar; Vitruvius; Strabo; and Pliny. See references to these authors (and to the Bible) within the text.

**Chapter 1. Egypt**

Casson, L. 1989. *Periplus Maris Erythraei.* Princeton: Princeton University Press.

Jones, D. 1990. *Boats*. London: British Museum Press.

Landström, B. 1970. *Ships of the Pharaohs.* New York: Doubleday.

Lipke, P. 1984. *Royal Ship of Cheops.* Oxford: BAR S. 225

Wachsmann, S. 1998. *Seagoing ships & Seamanship in the Bronze Age Levant.* College Station: Texas A & M University Press.

Ward, C.A. 2000. *Sacred & Secular: ancient Egyptian ships & boats.* Philadelphia:University of Pennsylvania

## Chapter 2. Arabia

Casson, L. 1989. *Periplus Maris Erythraei.* Princeton, Princeton University Press.

de Graeve, M. C. 1981. *Ships of the Ancient Near East.* Orientalia Lovaniensia Analecta 7. Katholieke Universiteit Leuven

Facey, W. & Martin, E.B. 1979. *Oman: A Seafaring Nation.* Muscat: Ministry of Information & Culture, Oman

Hourani, G.F. 1963. *Arab seafaring in the Indian Ocean in Ancient and Medieval Times.* Beirut Khayats. Repr. with notes, 1995. Princeton: Princeton University Press.

Pâris, F.E. 1843. *Essai sur la construction navale des peoples extra-européens.* Paris: Bertrand.

Tibbetts, G.R. 1971. *Arab Navigation in the Indian Ocean Before the Coming of the Portuguese.* Oriental Translation Fund NS42. repr. 1981. London: Royal Asiatic Society.

## Chapter 3. India

Arunachalam, B.1996. 'Traditional sea & sky wisdom of Indian seamen' In: Ray, H.P. & Salles, J-F. (ed) *Tradition & Archaeology*: 261- 81. Delhi: Manohar.

Deloche, J. 1994. *Transport & Communications in India prior to Steam Locomotion.Vol. 2 Water Transport.* New Delhi: O.U.P.

Greenhill, B. 1971. *Boats & Boatmen of Pakistan.* Newton Abbot: David & Charles.

Hornell, J. 1946. *Water Transport.* Cambridge: C.U.P. 2nd imp. 1970. Newton Abbot: David & Charles.

McGrail, S. *et al*, 2003. *Boats of South Asia.* London: Routledge-Curzon.

Pâris, F.E. 1843. *Essai sur la construction navale des peoples extra-européens.* Paris: Bertrand.

## Chapter 4. Australia
Anderson, A., Barrett, J.H. & Boyle, K.V. (ed) 2010. *Global Origins & Development of Seafaring.* Cambridge: McDonald Institute Monographs. esp. Chs 3 & 8.
Hornell, J. 1946. *Water Transport.* Cambridge C.U.P. repr. 1970. Newton Abbot: David & Charles.
Smith, M.A. Spriggs, M. & Frankhauser, B. (ed) 1993. *Sahul in Review.* Occ. Papers in Prehistory, 24. Canberra: Australian National University

## Chapter 5. South-East Asia
Aubaile-Sallenave, F. 1987. *Bois et bateaux du Viêtnam.* Ethnosciences 3. Paris:SELAF.
Horridge, G.A. 1978. *Design of Planked Boats of the Moluccas.* Monograph 38. Greenwich: National Maritime Museum.
Manguin, P-Y. 1985. 'Sewn plank craft of South-East Asia' in: McGrail, S & Kentley, E, (ed) *Sewn Plank Boats:* 319-344. Oxford: BAR S.276

## Chapter 6. China
Audemard, L. 1957-1969. *Les jonques chinoises.* Rotterdam: Maritiem Museum.
Donnelly, I.A. 1924. *Chinese Junks & other Native Craft.* Repr. 1988. Singapore: G. Brash
Mao, Y. (ed).1983. *Ancient China's Technology & Science.* Beijing: Foreign Languages Press
Peng, D. (ed). 1988. *Ships of China.* Beijing: Chinese Inst. of Navigation.
Worcester, G.R.G. 1966. *Sail & Sweep in China.* London: HMSO.
Zhang, S. 1991 (ed) *Proc. of the International Sailing Ships History Conference.* Shanghai: Soc. of Naval Architecture and Marine Engineering.

## Chapter 7. Oceania

Finney, B.R. 1994. *Voyages of Rediscovery.* Berkeley: University of California Press.

Haddon, A.C. & Hornell, J. 1936–1938. *Canoes of Oceania.* 3 vols. Honolulu: B.P. Bishop Museum. repub. as one volume, 1975.

Irwin, G. 1992. *Prehistoric Exploration & Colonisation of the Pacific.* Cambridge: C.U.P.

Lewis, D. 1994. *We the Navigators.* 2nd ed. Honolulu: University of Hawaii Press.

Pâris, F.E. 1843. *Essai sur la construction navale des peoples extra-européens.* Paris:Bertrand.

## Chapter 8. The Americas

Adney, E.T. & Chapelle, H.I. 1964. *Bark Canoes & Skin Boats of North America* Washington: Smithsonian Museum.

Edwards, C.R. 1965. 'Aboriginal watercraft on the Pacific coast of S. America.' *Ibero-Americáná*, 47. Berkeley & Los Angeles: University of California Press

Jablonski, N.G. (ed) 2002. *First Americans.* Memoirs of the California Academy of Sciences, 27. San Francisco.

Leshikar, M.E. 1988. 'Earliest watercraft: from rafts to Viking ships' in Bass, G (ed). *Ships & Shipwrecks of the Americas.* London: Thames & Hudson: 13-32

Pâris, F.E. 1843. *Essai sur la construction navale des peoples extra-européens.* Paris Bertrand.

Zimmerley, D.W. 1980. *Arctic kayaks.* Canadian Studies Report 11C. Ottawa: National Museums of Canada.

# Glossary

**Definitions of terms used in this volume.**

**Abeam**: on a bearing (direction) at right angles to the fore-and-aft line of the vessel.

**altitude:** angular height of a celestial body.

**aspect ratio (of a sail):** height$^2$ / area.

**azimuth:** horizontal, angular distance of a star from the north or south point of a meridian.

**Backstay:** an element of standing rigging supporting the mast, especially when the wind is abaft the beam. A line (sometimes a pair, port and starboard) running from mast head to stern. See also 'forestay' and 'shroud'.

**batten:** light strip of wood, similar to a lath.

**beam**: the beam of a vessel is her broadest breadth, usually at the waterline.

**beam-tie:** transverse strengthening member near the ends of a logboat.

**beating-spar:** spar used to keep taut the weather edge of a square sail.

**belay:** to make fast ('turn up') a line around a cleat or similar fitting.

**bevel:** surface that has been angled to make it fit with another.

**bilge:** region between sides and bottom of a boat.

**bipod:** mast with two legs.

**bireme:** oared vessel with two levels of oarsmen.

**bitts:** stout vertical posts to which lines and cables can be belayed.

**block:** a wooden case in which a sheave (a revolving wooden wheel) is fitted. Used to increase the 'handraulic' power applied to ropes, or to lead a rope in a convenient direction.(see also 'deadeye').

**boat:** a small, hollowed craft that derives buoyancy as water is displaced by the watertight hull.

**bole:** main stem or trunk of a tree.

**bonnet:** extra piece fastened to the foot of a sail to gain extra wind.

**boom:** spar to which the foot of a sail is bent. See also 'loose-footed'.

**bottom boards:** lengths of timber fastened together and laid over the bottom of a boat as a flooring.

**bowline:** a line to the bows from the luff (leading edge) of a square sail to keep the weather edge of the sail taut when a vessel is close hauled. See also 'tacking spar' and 'beating spar'.

**bowsprit:** a spar projecting forward of the stem of a ship to provide a fair lead for forestays. The bowsprit is held in position by lines (bowsprit shrouds) to each bow of the ship and by a bobstay to the ship's stem, just above the waterline.

**braces:** lines to the yard arms – used to trim the yard.

**brail:** rope used to bundle a sail thereby reducing its effective area.

**building sequence:** see 'frame-first' and 'plank-first'.

**building tradition:** an archaeological concept; the perceived style of building generally used in a certain region during a specified time range.

**bulkhead:** transverse partition dividing a vessel into compartments.

**buoyancy:** ability to float.

**Canted:** angled.

**capstan:** revolving barrel rotated about a vertical axis by long bars set within holes around its head; used to work cables and weigh anchor.

**carlings:** fore-and-aft timbers between crossbeams.

**catted:** an anchor is catted, rather than hoisted to the hawse pipe, when it is brought to a special timber (the cat head) where it hangs clear of the bow.

**caulk:** to insert material between two members thereby making the junction watertight.

**causeway:** a raised way across a stretch of water or other wet place.

**ceiling:** lining of planking over floor timbers and usually fastened to them.

**celestial pole:**  that point in the imaginary sphere in which the heavenly bodies lie, about which that sphere appears to rotate.

**chine:** the transitional region of a boat's hull where bottom and sides meet: 'hard chine'- when they meet at a pronounced angle; 'soft chine' when there is a gradual curve.

**clamp:** device for holding elements of a boat together (temporarily).

**cleat:** projection to which other fittings or a line are fastened.

**cleat rail:** longitudinal timber incorporating several cleats.

**clench:** deform, hook or turn the end of a nail fastening so that it will not draw out – may be done over a rove.

**clinker-built:** a form of boatbuilding in which the strakes are placed so that they partly overlap one another- usually upper strake outboard of lower, but, in South Asia, upper strake inboard of lower – see: 'reverse-clinker'.

**close-hauled:** sailing as close to the wind as is possible.

**coiled-basketry:** a method of linking together bundles of reeds in which individual bundles are not only themselves bound but also interlinked with other bundles.

**cotter:** a wooden pin that passes through a hole.

**couple:** pair of equal and parallel forces, acting in opposite directions and tending to cause rotation.

**cramp:** wooden fitting drawing together two timbers across a seam.

**crook:** curved piece of wood with the grain running along its length.

**crossbeam:** timber extending across a vessel.

**crutch:** a curved metal fitting on which an oar may be pivoted, or within which a spar may be housed.

**Day's sail:** the distance an 'average' ship, in the 'usual' conditions, could be expected to sail in 24 hours. Distances between ports were said to be 'X days' sail'.

**deadeye:** an elementary form of block with holes (rather than a sheave) through which ropes are rove to form a purchase.

**deadrise:** angle at which the bottom planking lies to the horizontal.

**deadweight:** the carrying capacity of a ship expressed in tonnes weight.

**departure (to take):** the last position of a ship, before losing sight of land, fixed from visual observation of landmarks.

**displacement:** the weight (tonnage) of water a ship displaces when afloat, at certain loaded states.

**double-banked:** said of oared boats when each oar is manned by two oarsmen.

**double-ended:** a vessel that is (nearly) symmetrical about the midships transverse plane.

**dowel:** piece of wood, rounded in cross section, used to secure a loose tenon or to join together two other wooden pieces.

**draft:** vertical distance between the waterline and the lowest point of a hull.

**drift:** a movement downwind caused by the wind acting on sail and hull.

**dunnage:** material, often wooden blocks, used to secure cargo in ships' holds.

**dutchman's log:** said to be used when speed is estimated by the time taken for a wood chip, dropped into the sea from the bow, to travel between two marks cut into the ship's gunwale.

**dynasty:** a succession of hereditary rulers.

**Expanded (said of a logboat):** after heat treatment (by sun, hot water; steam), the sides of a hollowed log are forced apart in a controlled manner, so that the breadth of the log near amidships increases, its midships height of sides decreases and its ends rise.

**extended (said of a logboat):** washstrakes are fastened to each side of a hollowed log so that the height of side is increased; this can compensate for the decrease in side height of a logboat that has been expanded. Rarely, logboats may be extended in length.

**Fetch:** distance of open water to windward of a stretch of coast.

**flare:** the transverse section of a boat increases in breadth towards the sheer.

**float:** a personal aid to flotation applied to the man partly immersed in the water.

**floor timber:** transverse member, often a crook, set against the bottom planking from turn of bilge to turn of bilge; may be abbreviated to 'floor' (see frame).

**flush-laid:** planking in which adjoining strakes are butted edge-to-edge. To be distinguished from clinker planking in which one strake partly overlaps the other.

**fore-and-aft sail:** sail generally set in or near the fore-and-aft line of a vessel.

**forefoot:** junction of stem and keel.

**forestay:** an element of standing rigging supporting the mast – running from mast head to the stem. See also 'backstay' & 'shroud'.

**frame:** transverse member set against the planking and made up of several timbers, usually a floor timber and a pair of futtocks. See also 'passive'.

**frame-first (skeleton–built):** form of boatbuilding in which the framework of keel, posts and frames is set up and fastened together before the planking is fashioned.

**framing-first:** form of boatbuilding in which keel, posts and elements of the lower framing are set up and fastened together before lower planking is fashioned and fastened to it ; followed by more (higher) framing, then more planking.

**freeboard:** height of sides above waterline.

**furled:** sails are said to be 'furled' when taken in and rolled up to their yard.

**futtocks:** elements of a frame; they support the side planking in a plank-first boat; in a frame-first boat, they define the shape of the lower hull. See: side timber.

**Galley:** vessel fitted for propulsion by oars and by sail.

**garboard:** strake next to the keel; the lowest side strake.

**girdle:** add additional planking at the waterline thereby increasing the vessel's waterline-beam measurement & therefore improving transverse stability; also known as 'furring'.

**girdled:** Egyptian vessel are said to have been 'girdled' when lines had been passed around the hull (horizontally or –towards the ends- vertically) to support the planking.

**grapnel:** a small anchor, for a boat rather than a ship.

**grommet:** strands of rope layed up in the form of a ring.

**guares:** retractable, wooden foil used to combat leeway and for steering; a variable lee- board.

**gudgeon:** an eyebolt on the sternpost, to receive the pintle of a rudder.

**Halyard:** line to hoist and lower yard and sail.

**hanging knee:** a vertical knee, below the structural member supported

**hatchway:** access via a hatch through the decks of a vessel.

**hog:** the bending or shearing of a hull in the vertical plane, causing it to arch upwards in the middle and to drop at the ends.

**hogging hawser or stay:** tensioned rope rigged on the centreline high in the hull to prevent hogging.

**hold:** a space within a hull for the stowage of cargo.

**hooked nail:** fastening nail that is clenched by turning its tip through 180°, back into the timber.

**hove-to:** underway, but not making way through the water.

**hulc:** a north-west European, medieval ship type, documented but not yet recognised in excavated remains.

**Informal harbour:** a natural landing place with little or no man-made improvements.

**interference fit:** said of a treenail in a hole, or of a tenon in its mortise, when the wood fibres interlock.

**Joggle:** to cut a notch in a timber so that it will fit close against another member.

**Keel:** main longitudinal strength member, joined to the fore-stem forward and the after-stem or sternpost aft.

**keelson:** centre-line timber above the floors, adding longitudinal strength and stiffness; may have a mast-step incorporated.

**knee:** naturally-grown crook used as a bracket between two members at about right-angles to each other. See: 'hanging knee', 'lodging knee' and 'standing knee'.

**knot:** one knot = one nautical mile per hour.

**Land breeze:** an evening/night wind that blows from land to sea when the land temperature falls below that of the sea.

**landfall:** in open seas, to sight and identify a point of land.

**landing place:** an un-improved site, suitable for vessels to 'take the ground', on riverbank or on a foreshore within a natural harbour.

**lap joint:** a form of wooden joint in which one part overlaps the other.

**lash:** to fasten together parts of a boat (two planks, a plank and frame etc) using cord or rope to make individual fastenings rather than continuous sewing.

**lath:** light, longitudinal batten placed over caulking to protect it, and held in place by fastenings.

**lateen:** triangular, fore-and-aft sail bent to a long yard

**leech:** the sides of a square sail, one being the weather leech, the other, the lee leech; in fore-and-aft rig the leach is the trailing edge of the sail.

**leeboard:** wooden board suspended over a boat's side to reduce leeway.

**lee platform:** term used to describe a feature of certain Oceanic sailing craft; used as a balance board from which to trim the craft.

**lee shore:** shore towards which predominant wind blows.

**leeway:** angular difference between a sailing vessel's fore-and-aft line and the direction actually made good; drift downwind.

**leeward:** away from the wind; the sheltered side; downwind.

**lift:** line running from yard arm to masthead, supporting the yard.

**limber hole:** notch cut in underside of frames to allow free circulation of bilge water.

**lines:** interrelation of sections in different planes which show the shape of a boat's hull; usually consist of sheer plan, half-breadth plan and body plan.

**lodging knee:** a horizontal knee.

**lofting floor:** a room or gallery with a large area of floor on which the full-scale lines of a vessel can be drawn.

**loll:** the state of a ship which is unstable when upright and therefore floats at an angle of heel, to one side or the other.

**loom:** that part of an oar inboard of pivot.

**loose-footed:** a sail without a boom at its foot.

**luff:** leading edge of a fore-and-aft sail.

**lug:** quadrilateral, fore-and-aft sail slung to leeward of the mast.

**Mast step**: fitting used to locate the heel of a mast; may be in keelson or floor timber.

**meridian:** 'line of longitude': a semi-great circle, crossing the equator and parallels of latitude at right angles, and joining the earth's poles.

**metacentre:** theoretical point (M) in the middle plane of a vessel through which the buoyancy force passes when the vessel is inclined at a small angle.

**metacentric height:** distance from the metacentre (M) to the centre of mass (G) of a loaded boat; a measure of a vessel's inherent stability.

**mizzen:** the aftermost mast of a three-masted vessel.

**mortise and tenon:** a method of fastening flush-laid planking in which free tenons are fitted into mortises cut in the edges of adjacent planks; after assembly, tenons may be pierced (locked) by two treenails, one in each plank. Formerly known as a 'draw-tongue joint'.

**moulded:** dimensions of a timber measured at right angles to the sided dimension.

**moulds:** transverse wooden patterns giving the internal shape of a vessel.

**nautical mile:** 1/60th of a degree on the equator: approx. 2,000 yards. one nautical mile (n.m.) approximately equals ten Roman stades.

**navigation:** generally: the art and science of taking a vessel safely and timely from one place to another. Within sight of land, pilotage methods are used.

**Oculus:** an eyelike design on each bow; the boat's 'eyes'.

**outrigger:** a counterpoising float rigged out from the side of a vessel to provide additional stability; some vessels have one on each side, others have a single outrigger which is mostly, but not always, kept to windward.

**Parbuckle:** a way of using a rope to raise or lower a cylindrical object, when it is impossible to use a purchase.

**paired boat:** a boat with two hulls, side by side, sometimes known as 'double-hull'.

**parrel:** a crook that holds a yard to the mast, yet allows the yard to pivot and to slide up and down the mast. See also 'trux' and 'ribs'.

**passage:** a single journey at sea by a vessel, either outward or homeward (see also 'voyage').

**passive (frame):** a frame that does not determine hull shape (as does an 'active' frame) but whose shape is determined by the form of the hull into which it is inserted.

**pay:** to cover a plank seam with hot pitch or coat a ship's bottom with a waterproofing substance.

**peak:** upper, after corner of a four-sided, fore-and-aft sail.

**petroglyphs:** rock art, graphic markings on a rock surface made for religious or other reasons. Sometimes known as 'pictographs'.

**pilotage:** the art of 'keeping the reckoning' (knowing the vessel's position) at sea when in sight of land.

**pintle:** metal pin on a sternpost on which the rudder hangs.

**plank:** component of a strake that is not all in one piece.

**plank-first (shell-built):** a form of boatbuilding in which the planking is (partly) erected and fastened together before framing is inserted.

**plank-keel:** a keel-like timber of which the ratio of its moulded dimension to its sided dimension is $< 0.70$.

**punted:** a form of propulsion in which a pole is used to push against sea or river bed.

**purchase:** a rope rove through two or more blocks, by means of which the force applied to the rope is increased, thereby moving heavy objects with less effort.

**Rabbet:** ('rebate') groove or channel worked in a member to accept another, without a lip being formed.

**raft:** buoyancy is derived from the flotation characteristics of each individual element (which must have a a specific density of less than 1).

**raked:** angled away from the vertical; also degree of overhang of a vessel's bow or stern.

**rays:** layers of parenchyma cells in horizontal strands running out from the centre of a tree towards the circumference.

**reach:** to sail with the wind from slightly forward of abeam to slightly aft.

**reef:** shorten sail by tying up the lower portion using reef points.

**reconstruction:** the establishment by logical processes of an excavated boat's original form, structure, propulsion and steering; hypothetical.

**reverse-clinker:** a form of boatbuilding in which strakes are laid so that an upper strake partly overlaps inboard of each lower strake.

**rib:** a simple form of frame; also laths in a parrel that keep the trux separate.

**ribband:** a flexible strip of wood, heavier than a batten, temporarily fastened to framing to assess fairness, and to establish the run of the planking.

**rigging:** standing rigging consists of all ropes supporting masts and yards; running rigging includes all ropes used for hoisting or sending down yards and for trimming sails to the wind.

**rocker:** fore-and-aft curvature of a keel or bottom of a vessel.

**rove:** washer-like piece of metal forced over the point of a nail before it is clenched.

**rowlocks:** a shaped space cut in a boat's gunwale to take an oar.

**run:** to sail with the wind from the stern sector.

**running rigging:** rigging used to hoist, lower or trim sails, or to hoist, brace or strike the yards. See: 'standing rigging'.

**Scarf**: tapered or wedge-shaped joint between pieces of similar section at the joint.

**scull:** a form of propulsion in which an oar is worked to and fro across the stern of a boat.

**sea breeze:** wind that blows from sea to land during the day, once the land temperature rises above that of the sea.

**seam:** juncture of two members required to be watertight.

**settee:** quadrilateral, lateen sail with a short leading edge.

**sewn:** a fastening that draws together two planks by the insertion of a thread through a series of holes; a continuous fastening, unlike a lashing which is an individual, isolated fastening.

**sheer; sheerline:** curve of the upper edge of the hull.

**shearing forces:** reversing forces within the hull of a planked vessel afloat that tend to make one part of the hull slide past the next, thereby seriously weakening plank fastenings and forcing caulking to drop out.

**sheer strake:** top strake of planking.

**sheet:** line used to trim foot of a sail.

**ship:** effectively, a very large boat.

**shore:** stout timber used to support hull of a vessel after she has taken the ground.

**shrouds:** an element of standing rigging, leading from masthead to sides of vessel to support mast athwartships. See also 'backstay' & 'forestay'.

**shunted:** specialised way of changing tack undertaken by a single outrigger boat that has her mast stepped amidships; after such a manoeuvre, the former stern becomes the bow.

**sided:** dimension of a timber measured (near) parallel to the fore-and-aft plane (or the keel) of a vessel.

**side timber:** framing timber supporting side planking at stations between floor timbers; may be adjacent to a floor but is not fastened to it.

**spile:** transfer a curved line onto a pattern which, when laid flat, will give the shape to cut a timber or a plank.

**spline:** a flexible strip of wood used to draw curves.

**sprit:** four-sided, fore-and-aft sail set on a sprit (spar) the lower end of which is made fast to the mast, while its upper end supports the peak of the sail.

**square sail:** four-sided sail, laced to a yard which generally lies square (at right angles) to the mast.

**stabilisers:** external longitudinal timbers fastened to a boat's sides at the loaded waterline to increase transverse stability. A similar effect is caused by 'furring'– see: girdle.

**stanchion:** a fixed, upright pillar supporting a vessel's deck.

**standing knee:** a vertical knee, above the structural member supported.

**standing rigging:** the fixed, permanent rigging supporting masts and yards.

**stays:** ropes leading from masthead forward and aft to support a mast.

**steerage way:** a vessel has steerage way when sufficient water passes over her rudder for it to be used to steer.

**strake:** a single plank or combination of planks stretching from bow to stern.

**stream:** the horizontal movement (ebb and flow) of water as tides rise and fall.

**stringer:** longitudinal strength member along inside of planking.

**sweep:** a long, heavy oar.

**swell:** an undulation that the sea retains for some time after a storm has ceased or a high wind has dropped.

**Tack:** (i). lower forward corner of a fore-and-aft sail. (ii). to alter course so that the bow of a sailing vessel passes through the wind.

**tacking spar:** a spar used to hold the weather leach of a square sail to the wind.

**taken aback:** when the wind bears against the forward face of the sail and the vessel is given sternway or is driven to leeward. Caused by an unexpected wind shift or an inattentive helmsman.

**tender:** said of a vessel inclined to heel well-over in a moderate breeze

**tenon:** piece of wood, rectangular in cross section, used to join timbers. May be an integral part of one timber, or may be 'loose', or 'locked' by a trans-piercing dowel.

**thole:** wooden pin projecting upwards at sheer level to provide a pivot for an oar.

**throat:** upper, forward corner of a four-sided. fore-and-aft sail.

**thwart:** transverse member (crossbeam) used as a seat.

**tidal range:** difference between height of high water and the next low water.

**timber:** generally, any piece of timber used in boatbuilding; one-piece ribs, especially those steamed or bent into shape, are known as 'timbers'.

**tradition:** 'boatbuilding tradition' is a conceptual tool, an archaeological/historical construct used to increase understanding: a perceived style of boatbuilding used in a specified region during a given period.

**transition strake:** strake at the transition ('chine') between bottom and side of a boat, especially where there is a marked change in the boat's transverse section.

**transom:** athwartship bulkhead, usually at the stern, occasionally at the bow.

**treenail:** hardwood peg, of multi-faceted section, with a head at one end and (sometimes) a wedge at the other. Used to join two members.

**trireme:** oared and sailed vessel with three levels of oarsmen.

**trux:** the several wooden balls in a parrel that facilitate movement around, and up and down, the mast.

**turned nail:** fastening nail clenched by turning the tip through 90° to lie along the face of the timber.

**tumblehome:** inboard inclination of the upper sides of a vessel; opposite of 'flare'.

**Volumetric coefficient**: ratio of displacement to the cube of waterline length: a measure of a vessel's speed potential.

**voyage:** journey made at sea, including both outward and homeward passages.

**Wale:** strake thicker than the others.

**washstrake:** an additional strake fitted to increase freeboard and to keep out spray and water.

**wear:** alter course by passing the stern of the sailing vessel through the wind.

**weather helm:** a vessel is said to 'carry weather helm' when the tiller has to be kept to windward to counteract the vessel's tendency to come up into the wind.

**windlass:** similar to a capstan, but on a horizontal shaft.

**windward:** the side from which the wind blows; opposite of leeward.

**Yard:** spar suspended from a mast and to which the head of a square sail (or the luff of a triangular sail) is bent.

**yardarm:** the ends of a yard, to which braces are made fast.

**Zenith:** highest point of a heavenly body's trajectory.

**Note**. Where dimensions of vessels are noted (e.g.12 x 4 x 2 m.) they are given in the order: Length overall; maximum Breadth (usually at the waterline, amidships); Depth of hull amidships.

# Index

Notes 'W.T' = Water Transport:  float, raft, boat or ship
'boatbuilding' includes 'shipbuilding'